Practical Personnel
Policies
For Small Business

Practical Personnel
Policies
For Small Business

Theodore Cohn   *Roy A. Lindberg*

An Inc./Van Nostrand Reinhold Publication

VAN NOSTRAND REINHOLD COMPANY
NEW YORK CINCINNATI TORONTO LONDON MELBOURNE

Material in pages 109–111 adapted from *Secrets of a Corporate Headhunter,* by John Wareham, with the permission of Atheneum Publishers. Copyright © 1980 The Wareham Family Trust.

Copyright © 1984 by Inc. Publishing Corporation

Library of Congress Catalog Card Number 82–20696

ISBN: 0–442–21699–8

Manufactured in the United States of America

Published by Van Nostrand Reinhold Publishing
135 West 50th Street, New York, N.Y. 10020

Van Nostrand Reinhold
480 Latrobe Street
Melbourne, Victoria 3000, Australia

Van Nostrand Reinhold Company Limited
Molly Millars Lane
Wokingham, Berkshire, England

Macmillan of Canada
Division of Gage Publishing Limited
164 Commander Boulevard
Agincourt, Ontario M1S 3C7, Canada

15 14 13 12 11 10 9 8 7 6 5 4 3 2 1

Library of Congress Cataloging in Publication Data

Cohn, Theodore.
    Practical personnel policies for small business.

    Includes index.
    1. Personnel management.   2. Small business.
I. Lindberg, Roy A.   II. Title.
HF5549.C545 1983   658.3'03   82–20696
ISBN 0–442–21699–8

Contents

Preface

This book will be of most use to you if you understand from the outset that it is *not* a complete treatise on personnel. Many books cover personnel management in companies of all sizes. This book covers the personnel practices unique to the smaller company— defined as the organization below $50 million in annual sales, a line we have arbitrarily drawn since there is no clear or commonly accepted boundary between smaller and larger firms.

Smaller companies have special opportunities in and problems of personnel management almost entirely related to their size. Whom they attract, how they select, what they offer, how jobs are defined and changed, how their people know what is expected of them, how they evaluate performance, how a team is built, and how people are terminated cannot be handled in smaller companies as they are in larger firms.

Because most of what is printed in business journals and taught in business schools is based on the experience of larger companies, it is sometimes difficult for the manager in a smaller company to know which techniques will work for *him*. This book attempts to zero in on the aspects and techniques of personnel management that are size related. It will be facts and experience based, using examples from our managing, consulting, and speaking experiences.

Several prejudices underlie the content of the book. One is that the basic personality, the strengths and weaknesses of a person, is hard to change. We doubt that managers have the right to try to change it. Skills can be learned: the debits are here, the credits there; this is a hammer, that a chisel. You can teach people to read and to listen and to plan and set wage scales. But we question whether you can significantly affect the ability people have to initiate, to be sensitive to the needs of others, to handle stress, and to be comfortable in different types of personal relationships.

Although the working environment over which you have control affects behavior, we feel that it is usually a bad economic investment for the smaller company manager to try to change the basic personality of her employees. Better to define what the job needs in the way of personal strengths and weaknesses and then hire properly. We say: Spend about ten times more time and money hiring people than training them. That is a practical thought for the smaller company where all assets are usually in short supply, especially the most valuable—the time of its key people. That time should be devoted to selecting the best people, not to training or bolstering those who are selection errors.

Another prejudice is that we believe people cannot and should not be manipulated. The "cannot" is based on the practicality of the individuality, self-protectiveness, and orneriness of the human personality; the "should" is a moral conclusion. We have been asked to design compensation programs which were supposed to get people to produce more or the same for less money. Because we felt that the goal was both immoral and impractical, we have turned down such requests. Thus, the book will not show you how to take advantage of employees, but how to get more from them by paying more. It assumes that production can increase, that people will do more for the company—if they know they will get more. "More" need not be money—although in many cases it is and should be. "More" may be recognition, promotion, freedom, or anything else seen as a reward by the people involved.

Our experience has shown that the great bulk of smaller company managers are trying to do the right thing, that they are looking for approaches to improving not only the profits of their companies but the working conditions and quality of life of their employees. We have written the book to be responsive to their search.

One more of our prejudices is that the personnel function should serve overall management objectives. It does not contribute when it stands by itself. That means you should have a clear and well-founded, market-based strategy before reviewing or designing your personnel policies. *No policy is useful that does not direct behavior toward the creation and maintenance of advantages in the marketplace.*

To achieve efficiency, companies must give a clear message to their people so they can know on their own what they should do in what priority order, and no message can be clearer than one based on a strategy aimed at creating market advantages. We assume that you have or will develop such a strategy. This book is not a text on how to set strategy, but on how to improve implementation of strategy through strong, consistent, and integrated policies.

We believe that the quality of personnel management and profitability are intertwined. Companies which are strong and enjoying above-average profitability through time are distinguished by two characteristics. One is their unique market or service advantages, the things which make it desirable for a customer to do business with them. The other is the efficiency with which they use their human resources. Whom you hire and retain and how you direct their behavior is directly tied to the marketing advantages you will create or miss. Personnel practices support the marketing advantages or they do not. Because the smaller firms tend to pay inadequate attention to the personnel function, they tend also not to realize the point and make use of the practices. We will deal with the connection between practices and the advantages more fully later on.

Last among our prejudices relevant to this book is our conviction that personnel management in the smaller firm is most influenced by the value or ethical system of the firm's key people. Since the values are seldom explicitly stated (personnel manuals rarely touch on them), we will explore some simple ways for you to determine what your feelings are on key issues which directly affect personnel management. Financial statement disclosure, sharing of profits in excess of corporate needs, willingness to share decisions and ownership are sensitive issues, more deeply affected by values than by personnel pronouncements.

One final comment is necessary before this preface is complete: This is not a book about the personnel *function*. It is a book about personnel *management*. How the singular expression came into being we do not know, but it is as odious as it is common. The degree of its usage is, in our opinion, a sound measure of the degree to which the "filing-cabinet syndrome" preempts genuine efforts to employ people in accordance with the best of their and organizational interests.

Acknowledgments

Many people helped us in writing this book. In addition to those listed who made specific contributions, we want to thank our clients who showed us in how many ways successful companies can handle their personnel and gave us a chance to try some of our ideas. The following people were generous in sharing their experiences:

Paul B. Barringer, President, Coastal Lumber Company

David P. Blackshear, President, Atlanta Dental Supply Company

Donald R. Calman, President, Printcraft Systems, Inc.

John E. Cross, President, Elphinstone, Inc.

Dr. Cyril Franks, University Professor, Graduate School of Applied and Professional Psychology, Rutgers University

Douglas F. Glant, President, Pacific Group

Charles R. Kimmel, Chairman, Kimmel Automotive, Inc.

Rolfe I. Kopelan, President, Human Resource Management, Inc.

Howard E. Kraft, President, Climate Control, Inc.

R. E. Lind, President, Crystal Farms, Inc.

Peer Lorentzen, President, Chem-Trend Incorporated

William A. Mason, Vice-President, The Goodyear Bank

Thomas M. Pfaff, President, Spartan Equipment Company

Murray Raphel, President, Gordon's Alley

Vincent A. Riggio, President, Frank D. Riggio Co., Inc.

Samuel B. Shapiro, Samuel B. Shapiro Consulting, Inc.

H. H. Stith, Jr., President, Stith Equipment Company

James T. Tanner, President, Tanner Companies, Inc.

Laurence Taylor, Hillsdale, Michigan

William J. Willmot, President, Harmony Castings, Inc.

We also want to thank Brenda Lindberg and Irene Graf for their help in preparing the manuscript and correcting errors and mistakes where we were sure there were none.

1 ❧
Keys to Understanding the Personnel Function

Since industrialization began, personnel has been treated as a resource with fixed characteristics and little capacity for change. As a result, it received far less attention than other resources.

The situation has changed. "People are our most important asset" is the popular theme today. And for once, popularity has a basis in fact. Personnel costs are the largest or second largest costs in most companies. They are also usually the largest controllable cost, even in non-labor-intensive organizations.

Under conditions of intensifying world-wide competition and increasingly differentiated productivity, it is no longer safe to be casual about personnel management. Many larger companies have learned that lesson and are spending millions to get more out of their people. Smaller companies cannot afford to do relatively less. The firms that survive will be those that bring attention to personnel up to the level given to financial and material assets.

In this chapter we present the factors that bear on the personnel policies and practices of all companies, whatever their size.

Personnel as a Profit Source

Personnel management deserves a high place among organizational concerns because in most companies it is the richest source of potential increases in productivity and profit. A personnel manager of a company known for its technological pioneering highlighted that point by saying: "The input-output relationship of our developing more productive machinery is microscopic compared to what we can gain from increased involvement, ideas, and productivity of our people using the old machines." Further support is provided by the reasons behind superior corporate performance. Personnel practices are a leading source of profits.

A bitter lesson is being learned by U.S. industry: the key to profitability is no longer through industrial engineering. True, industrial engineering has always taken the human factor into consideration, but always as a variable involved in *the process.* Anything that benefited the process—better lighting, higher or lower seats, armrests, shorter reaches, color-coding—but nothing that benefited the people in the form of opportunities to derive satisfaction from work was done. Benefits to people were incidental to the interest of industrial engineering. That disinterest contributed to the steady erosion in productivity gains and quality of production that led to the oceans of red ink in which so many of our major industries are swimming today.

In an earlier book we pointed out that success in business depended upon three minimal accomplishments—the provision of:

1. wanted products
2. lean costs
3. worker satisfaction[1]

All three are required for success and they are highly interdependent. Products made at low costs by dissatisfied workers or made at high costs by satisfied workers will not be wanted for long—assuming they were wanted in the first place.

The story of General Motors' Corvair supports the foregoing premise. To combat imports, GM set about designing a car that would offer a little more of everything imported vehicles had but that would also sell at approximately the same price. And they succeeded. The Corvair had a little more power, space, and style than equivalent imports—and the car was wanted (it sold well). But GM did not earn

[1]Cohn and Lindberg, *Survival & Growth: Management Strategies for the Small Firm,* New York: AMACOM, 1974.

a cent from the car during its production lifetime. Why? Because in meeting the second requirement for success (lean costs), GM built a new factory at Lordsville, Ohio, in which every operation that could be economically automated was automated. The work that was too expensive to automate was given to people to do. You can imagine what kind of work that was—work in tight corners, complex work, and work in making things fit together that did not fit together as they should—work just as routine as that taken over by machines but more demanding. The result was great dissatisfaction with the work and quality so poor that the car had the most doleful rate-of-repair record of any GM car.

The lesson is clear: to be lastingly successful in business, the three elements are required. If one is missing, success is beyond reach. Personnel is as important as any resource and more important than most resources.

CULTURAL FACTORS

In shaping personnel management policies and plans, you should take into account factors in the economic and social world that affect the success of your personnel program. Some of the factors are: de-emphasis on growth; growing emphasis on individualism; increasing professionalism at higher work levels; onset of permanent inflation; and rising incidence of family employment.

De-emphasis on growth. The slowing of U.S. economic growth and rising doubt about the desirability of growth have increased the value of job security over career growth.

Growing emphasis on individualism. Most managers are moving away from group thinking. The movement toward individualism has been most pronounced among bright, youthful executives and technicians. Unemployment protection programs have helped shift people's concerns from earning a living to doing a job one prefers. The result has been that good people now have choices in jobs, lifestyles, and places to live, choices which were previously available only to a few.

Many young managers are conscious of a conflict between what they want out of their lives and what being successful in corporate terms demands. In seeking to resolve the conflict they often ask themselves such questions as:

"How much loyalty do I owe the company if it won't allow me to live as I want to?"

"Can I live with myself when I compromise my code of ethics and
   my integrity?"

The answers that come back increasingly favor lifestyle over institutional success.

Increasing professionalism at higher work levels. The definition of
a professional has expanded beyond the traditional doctor, lawyer,
and accountant roles to include younger managers who see their
loyalties primarily to themselves and their work. Personnel policies
need to reflect that fact. That means pay should be negotiated rather
than dictated and that making decisions that affect individual development and careers should be shared.

Onset of permanent inflation. Inflation has become an integral part
of base pay. Most companies routinely raise salary levels to match
inflation. But, doing so has limited value. It is better to raise individual
salaries to market levels than to make across-the-board adjustments
in proportion to inflation. Raising individual salaries increases your
chances of keeping good performers and losing poor ones.

Rising incidence of family employment. The percentages of women
working and the number of families with two or more wage earners
are increasing. More employees are concerned with the careers of
other working family members and are less willing to accept promotion opportunities or working conditions that require relocation
or have a negative effect on family life.

PSYCHOLOGICAL FACTORS

Once employees get above the subsistence level represented by unemployment benefits, Social Security, and welfare, the degrees to
which their security and job-satisfaction needs are met are determined
largely by how their employers treat them, their firm's economic
success and standing in the community, the challenge of their jobs,
and other factors specific to their firms. But even more influential
are factors specific to them, the psychological factors commonly dealt
with in business circles under the phrase "attitudes toward work."
   All personnel programs are based on assumptions about the nature
of people—that people generally are lazy, careless, and selfish, or
that they are hardworking, caring, and social. These assumptions
convey management's views about employees' willingness to work.
Programs in companies with negative views of willingness to work
favor procedural control over self-control, stress the exercise of authority over its delegation, and promote managers' benefits over

worker development. Programs in companies with positive views about employees' willingness to work reverse those positions. While no survey has ever been made to prove the relationship between positive views about employees and corporate profitability, what evidence there is strongly suggests that profits are higher in firms with positive views.

An article in the May 11, 1981, issue of *Business Week,* "The New Industrial Relations," commented on the willingness-to-work issue. It asserted what some managers have intuitively believed for a long time—that most people want to work and will be productive if they have the proper financial, psychological, and social incentives.

Of course, people cannot be treated as though they all have the same attitudes toward work, and personnel programs that rest on the assumption that they do are wrong. Much more important than whether people really want to work is the question why people work. The answers to the second question are many. But knowing what the answers are and in what proportion tells a lot about the incentives an employer can create.

Currently, an estimated 40 percent of the workforce holds new work values. One group rejects money as a substitute for personal fulfillment. They are the "free souls" who find it difficult to fit into formal job and organizational structures. Another group works primarily to earn money, not for its own sake, but to buy a lifestyle. Neither group can be effectively managed using traditional values.

That observation was given support by the May 11 *Business Week* article, which stated flatly, "One of the most dehumanizing assumptions ever made is that workers work and managers think." In rejecting that assumption, the article makes a strong plea for exploring participative management techniques, such as Quality of Work Life programs. We side with the plea. There is a need for exploration in the field of personnel management in every company.

Participation can both benefit an enterprise and harm it. We have observed that participative management is widely practiced in almost all exceptionally profitable enterprises, but that it has failed in most others. Participatory programs usually fail for lack of support. Many managers resent giving up the control they have fought so long to attain, and would fight equally hard against admitting the resentment. The result is an environment in which genuine participation has no chance to get started, much less to prevail.

ORGANIZATIONAL FACTORS

Knowing worker attitudes, the changes taking place in them, and what other firms are doing about them is important to firms that want to have effective personnel programs. But that knowledge does not constitute the whole of the foundation for effective personnel management. Also needed is self-knowledge, that is, knowledge of the organization's inner dynamics and character. Personnel management can never be effective in firms without this understanding.

Each firm lives in accordance with certain values and resources in an external world, which decides its survival and profitability. No firm can do more to assure its future than to identify needs in the external world and fill them uniquely. That feat is much more difficult to accomplish than most people realize, cope as the firm must with the constraints of its values and resources. But the firm that does not succeed in removing the barriers to filling needs in the outer world does not survive the average corporate lifetime of six to seven years (our estimate).

You may recall our saying earlier that intelligent personnel management generates competitive advantages. It does so by meeting the growing and explicit demand of workers at all levels for higher satisfaction from their work. Acknowledging that demand and creating the environment to satisfy it is not only a challenging task, but a competitively advantageous one. It raises productivity and quality of output and lowers costs and customer dissatisfactions.

The key to creating a satisfying work environment is self-knowledge: knowledge within the firm of why customers buy from it and why they do not, what the firm is doing that keeps it in business, what it is doing that threatens its future, how it keeps in touch with and what it does about changes in the outside world, why employees stay with the firm and why they leave, and much more knowledge that is rarely found in companies.

The smaller company is in a good position to understand itself. The key to achieving such understanding lies in stripping the enterprise to its basic dynamics and assembling them in a model. The next step, or course, is to feed alternate scenarios (that is, contrasting sets of data) into the model in a search for optimal results—the behavioral pattern that pays off best in its interaction with the real world.

The job does not end there, of course. There is the matter of looking ahead. Few companies of any size understand clearly where they can and want to be in two or three years. But, in any company that wants to manage its human resources effectively, someone has to sort out what the firm wants to accomplish before he can begin meaningful work on personnel policies, including a compensation plan.

We are not talking of a sophisticated financial model, which is a common tool in financial planning, but of a simple model built around market uniqueness.

The process of building the model may be problematic, mainly a result of overcomplicating it with gratuitous assumptions. Start with a clean slate: keep all assumptions out except those you simply cannot operate without. Then, ask questions such as:

"Why do people buy from us?"

"Is our business vulnerable to major discontinuities—technological breakthroughs, government-imposed bans?"

"What do we have to do especially well to succeed?"

"What do customers not like about any firm in the industry?"

From these general questions, it is possible to move to the development of a model of the business.

In companies with genuine and actionable uniqueness, clear and specific enough that their managers know how to spend their discretionary time, everyone understands that promotions are given to reward support and enhancement of the uniqueness, people are let go when they reduce it, chief executive officers (CEOs) spend most of their time monitoring it, meeting agendas are built around it, and training and selection focus on supporting it.

Limitations of Self-Understanding

Knowing your culture, your people, and your organization is not all there is to personnel management. There are other realities to be considered, some of which we can see for ourselves and some of which we cannot. Time and time again we have seen companies that exhibit responsible attitudes and high energy with respect to human resources make serious mistakes in developing their programs and policies. The mistakes were made because these companies never saw themselves as they really were.

Nor can they ever. No organization can fully understand itself or fix its shortcomings. For that, outside help is needed. Smaller firms have special needs for such help since the variety of internal perspectives and influences in them is necessarily smaller than in larger firms and the dry rot of group-think is more likely to be present in them. Yet, on the average, smaller firms use outside help less frequently than larger firms do.

Personnel specialists from the larger consulting firms do not bang on the doors of smaller corporations as often as they do on those of larger corporations. Even if they did, there are real questions whether they are the best for smaller firms. They are usually too driven to create billings to get to know your company as well as they will need to to serve it intelligently without incurring uncomfortably high costs.

Personnel specialists who can know your firm well are available on a long-term, part-time basis from many sources. Among sources are moonlighters from larger companies and local professors with consulting experience. For example, a colleague of ours, the head of the psychology department of a local university, has worked with clients of ours and his own in all of the twenty years we have known him.

The value of having a professional, regular part-time consultant is that:

1. She is current in the personnel field (as you probably are not).
2. She gets to know the organization (as you cannot).
3. She can get rid of demotivating practices (before you do and before they become destructive).

A part-time personnel expert can bring into the company new ideas on employee development, motivation, incentives, executive salary levels, organizational structure, comparative costs of fringe benefits, and many other factors bearing on human resources.

The cost of such professionalism in most cases will be paid back many times by higher productivity, better hirings (more competence for the money or less money for the competence needed), fewer dissatisfactions over benefits, and a reduction in turnover.

The Main Obstacle to Constructive Human Employment

Perhaps the most powerful among the factors impinging on personnel management (in the United States at least) is the dichotomy between labor and management that has almost constitutional status in this country. No progress can be made in managing human resources until the stumbling block of the adversary relationship between the two is recognized and removed.

Removing it will be an enormous task, because to most Americans the principle of adversary relationships is the very image of the system that has made the country rich. People believe that the outputs of our society arise ultimately from the efforts of opposing forces held in balance by the weights of discrete interests. When output falters, as it has done recently in the automobile industry, the fault is laid at the door of politics. But the late arrival of U.S.-made, fuel-efficient vehicles in the marketplace and the poor quality of American-built cars were not a result of tax structures or unregulated foreign competition. They were a result of the we-they, I-win-you-lose mentality that weighs down American productivity.

Management experimentation in the free world shows that adversary relations are of little or no benefit to production or consumption. Increasingly, the experimentation demonstrates that the ultimate increases in efficiency come from united rather than adversary behavior. The Swedish, German, and Japanese situations are examples of that united behavior.

Americans may feel they have heard enough comparisons with Japanese management techniques—comparisons in which the Japanese always seem to come out ahead. We think there are lessons in the Japanese experience that are applicable to the smaller company personnel manager in this country. To make them clear, we have to address the American management win-lose, adversary relationship in which those being paid a salary are in opposition to those paying the salary. The win-lose relationship is simple: I make more money if you work harder and I pay you no more or, if I can get fewer of you to do the job, I benefit. In every case, we are on opposite sides of the profit table—my gain is your loss and vice versa. The manager cannot win that battle, nor can the worker. In a competitive society, only the winning *company* provides security and satisfaction to the worker and manager and survival and profit to the owner. The manager who alienates his employees by winning a short-term salary or work condition argument and the worker who produces less than competitive workers will both destroy the company and their jobs.

The Japanese (and, in our view, progressive managers everywhere) take the position that workers are not only assets, but also a principal source of ideas for change and improvement. Who knows better how to improve the product, cut the cost, reduce the paperwork, or speed up the flow of product and information than the people doing the job? There is also, of course, the social contract that exists in Japan, which implies the organization has moral responsibility for the care of its people beyond providing them with a job. Let us omit social value from our discussion, because it is foreign to most Americans. But the idea that the person doing a job is in the best position to improve it is practical enough to appeal to American egalitarian instincts.

Size bears directly on the capacity to use personal relationships to practical advantage. Managers of smaller companies can more directly show employees that they count and will be listened to than can managers in larger companies, who must depend much more on institutional procedures to get across the same message. However, small firms can not assume that their simpler structure and small size offer an inherent competitive advantage in their personnel relationships. The size of a firm alone does not affect job satisfaction. When industry characteristics and individual factors such as age and marital status are excluded, morale is independent of the size of the firm. Also, in a smaller firm, a strong, dominating person is more likely to use people, in the exploitative sense, because it has few or no institutional limits on personnel practices.

American managers often act as if people are unpredictable. They know machines can be programmed and controlled with reasonable accuracy. But because people are individual, hard to understand, and cannot be programmed, managers apply more redundant and tighter controls over people than they do over machines. Without the controls, people are likely to mess up things. This view moves people from being assets to being liabilities.

Progressive companies have learned that results largely dependent on people are predictable—*if* the responsibility for the results is clearly given to the people doing the work. We have sufficient hard evidence that teams can work with minimum direct supervision if they understand clearly what they are supposed to do. The supervisor's role becomes that of providing information, coaching, and clarifying the boundaries of responsibility between the working group and the rest of the organization.

If a personnel policy assumes that behavior is predictable and group skills are valuable, promotion will be based on the new standards, and raises and bonuses will be used to reward participatory skills as well as production and financial results. Management has to respond quickly to suggestions and grievances. Work improvement programs will probably fail if their sole goal is more production or better worker feelings. Successful programs require a hardheaded balance between job satisfaction and better productivity. Remember that everyone is not ready for innovative work relationships. Give those who feel uncomfortable the chance of not joining but still belonging.

Negative Effects of Accounting Practices

One of the conventions of accounting interferes with thinking about and employing people as assets, that is, as resources which have value beyond the immediate accounting period, generally a year. Conventional treatment does not look upon employees as assets and, consequently, writes off all personnel costs in the current year.

Managers who think of personnel as assets and spend large amounts in selecting, training, developing, and supporting personnel are faced every accounting period with the fact that all personnel efforts end up as costs in the present; nothing shows on the balance sheet for the future value of the human organization. That fact makes the performance of investing in people look pretty bad in the eyes of short-term thinkers, and handicaps efforts to gain acceptance for long-range personnel programs.

Most managers agree that people perform better when they are held accountable—the inventory manager does a better job when she knows that specific outage and turnover statistics are being used to measure her performance, the CEO when he knows his company's performance is being compared against industry statistics. In each case, performance is measurable and explicit, and if the standards are not achieved, the individual knows to what extent.

Application of these views of accountability and management to the human organization is handicapped by the fact that we have, in common practice, no way of saying on an objectively underpinned basis to a manager, "here are the human assets for which you are responsible, here is what we expect you to do with them and the condition in which we expect you to return them to us at the end of the year, here is the standard which determines what an exceptional job in managing those assets will be." Therefore, one of the goals in personnel management is the sensitizing of managers to the asset of the human organization, an especially critical task in the smaller company because of the smaller number of key people required to make the organization successful. The smaller the number of people, the greater the chances of one individual's views dominating—in which situation personnel seldom achieve asset stature.

In the last fifteen years there has been a movement to quantify the human organization by putting people on the balance sheet. To some critics, the attempt is demeaning; by lumping people with money and inventories, we make them objects. But we do not agree. When someone is held accountable for an asset, he is likely to deal with it more respectfully.

Proponents of the attempt to quantify the human organization have pointed out that we treat dollars more skillfully than we treat human assets. We should be as skilled in managing people as we are in managing finances! The consequences of skillful personnel management are not merely more dollars of profit; they are, more importantly, an increase in happiness at work.

Human resources accounting, the name of the technique that formally treats employees as assets, was started by psychologists who felt that, after they agreed on the accounting for certain personnel costs such as hiring and turnover, managers could gradually move into such non-auditable areas as the value of the human organization.

We will touch on some of the costs of acquiring and losing people, but will stay clear of the difficult issue of computing the future value of individuals, a subject that is still being challenged theoretically.

Simply, if a sales manager is given the responsibility for a $300,000 asset, he is likely to pay attention to it. That is the cost of acquiring a twenty-person sales organization in a distribution business. By assigning a dollar value to the costs of hiring, training, and developing sales people to a productive level, the CEO makes it clear to the sales manager that he is as responsible for the $300,000 sales organization as the inventory manager is for the $4 million inventory.

2 ❧
Creating the Climate for Effective Personnel Management

Much of the writing about personnel management leaves the impression that among other corporate activities it is a stand-alone function—that what it does and how it operates are determined primarily by externals such as legislation, economic conditions, industry practices, and the like. But the opposite is true. Personnel management is a function very much under the influence of other corporate activities. In fact, the ultimate determinant of the way a firm's human resources are managed is the way the firm manages itself overall. A firm that manages itself poorly manages its people poorly.

In this chapter we offer some guidelines to creating the climate within which a vital, contributing personnel function can flourish.

Key Features of Good Management

Examination of the character of good managements then, will yield clues as to the character of good personnel management. Effective management has four key characteristics. Effective management is:

demanding

consistent

performance-aware

rewarding

Let's take a closer look at each item.

DEMANDING MANAGEMENT

Good management is demanding of all its resources, extracting from each kind its full contribution to the organization, and people are no exception. Therefore, any practice that reduces demand on employees is bad practice.

We have never met a good, undemanding manager. Our experience tells us there is almost a linear relationship between managerial effectiveness and the weight of demand put on people. We define demand as:

1. an obligation to perform beyond the routine laid upon an employee, which
2. requires her to operate at the outer edges of her capacities.

When the demands are realistic and made in acceptable ways, they almost always produce the results sought.

People respect their accomplishments in proportion to their difficulty, and people's self-respect is largely derived from personal measures of performance. The employee who admires himself for unexceptional accomplishments, even when others see them as exceptional, is rare. Therefore, few people who have been driven to more fully utilize their capabilities ever curse their drivers. The "Boy, I'm fagged; that so-and-so's really been busting my butt" kind of comments usually hide a good deal of pride in accomplishment.

CONSISTENT MANAGEMENT

The next word on the list of characteristics of effective management—consistent—refers to the fact that good management fosters internal consistency, a harmony of goals, needs, work, and values. Organizations that take these factors into account in managing their affairs are much more productive than organizations that do not. True, employees in either kind of company know what to expect— but different expectations yield different results.

To manage in preservation of consistency, as well as to manage consistently, you will have to understand your corporate culture. That understanding has to be part of your plans for change, especially for implementing change. A plan that violates the visible or hidden corporate culture is almost sure to fail through direct opposition or gentle sabotage.

For example: A cost-conscious, secretive paper distributor grew up believing that the only way to make money was to assume that everyone wanted something for nothing. He could not bring himself to install a compensation system set with the participation of employees because it required disclosure of some financial information that, he was convinced, would raise the pay demands of his employees. He continued to lose his good people and to have difficulty replacing them.

In a second case, a manufacturer of high-precision, imaginatively engineered, small-lot equipment failed when he tried to shift to making lower quality consumer goods on a mass basis. The deeply rooted values, norms, and expectations of his employees conflicted with the mechanics of routinely producing products viewed as mundane and low quality.

In a third case, the corporate culture had been to milk present profits. It took a long time for executives to reach the top. When they did, they were of an age when it seemed sensible to follow their predecessors' example: take out of the company all currently available earned cash. A plan to invest current profits in the future was offered. It could not be openly opposed by the older managers; the plan was motherhood. But these managers effectively blocked the plan by finding something to question about every new item presented and asking for more information before deciding. What with client assignments, the difficulty of getting people together, and dealing with questions about the information provided, no change was approved.

Companies can be dominated by maintainers, by high-risk takers, by aggressive tigers interested in growth and status, or by pussy cats interested in avoiding decision, but never by people who are at odds with the internal culture. Each manager can affect the corporate culture, but only as fast as the culture will permit and that is never fast in anybody's language. Since an existing culture is primarily a function of the collective content of the minds of the employee body, changes in the culture cannot be made arbitrarily.

PERFORMANCE-AWARE MANAGEMENT

The third in the list of characteristics of effective management is performance-awareness. Good managers always know how well their people are doing and how their performance compares with that of competitors. A good manager knows, generally, by instinct or intuition, but never leaves it at that. Periodically she submits her subjective appraisals to test, using analytical methods to confirm or correct them.

Keeping abreast of the quality of performance is critical to personnel management. It is impossible to reward employees equitably, much less manage them intelligently, when performance is not measured and known. Effective training, development, career-planning, staffing, and more depend upon performance evaluation.

REWARDING MANAGEMENT

Last among the characteristics of effective management is that it is rewarding. This characteristic follows from demands and performance-awareness Demands cannot be laid upon personnel consistently unless rewards are given for meeting them; appropriate and equitable rewards cannot be paid without objective performance appraisal.

Values, Norms, and Management Styles

All management styles are expressions of values or norms, which are the expectations and ways of doing things that exist in almost all human groups. We are all culturally conditioned to some extent by individual backgrounds and environmental influences.

There is no way to avoid norms. Whether or not we like them, we have weather conditions; and in organizations we have norms. The manager in an organization is often unaware of the norms, especially if he is a key person, one of those responsible for creating and supporting them. The analogy to the fish being unaware of the water in which it lives is appropriate.

Norms do not arise in a vacuum. Whatever the size of the firm, norms arise from the founder or from the person who made the firm big. The success of ITT is ascribed to the financial discipline and careful operating plans Harold Geneen created. Exxon originally left the entrepreneurial managers of its acquired office equipment businesses free to run their operations, accepting a management style different from that practiced in the world's largest oil company. The acquired managers negotiated Board control with one proviso: Exxon could exercise its majority stock ownership only by monitoring capital infusions or by throwing out the original entrepreneurs. IBM symbolizes customer-service concern with a twenty-four-hour hot line and top management visits in the field to check service. Avis and

Pepsi used their number two market positions as a competitive stimuli. J. C. Penney still expresses its founder's concern for people.

A manager has to know about the existence of his firm's norms and their strength before he can effectively change the behavior of his people, implement personnel policies, or increase the participation, input, and commitment of employees. Behavior of employees is largely determined by the norms applied to openness, risk-taking, willingness to experiment, errors, past successes, information sharing, decisions, and profits.

We are not proposing that a company is healthier when it is monolithic in its conformity. A monolithic culture will inevitably lead to corporate death. Although different currents run through an organization, there are usually predominant ones that determine how things are done, what can be discussed, what counts, and who is recognized and rewarded. Smaller organizations can be mobilized toward positive goals more quickly and surely than larger ones can. If top management wants to change the signals it sends out, it can do so more efficiently in a small company: the lines of communication are shorter and less likely to be distorted.

The areas most affected by norms have been well summarized by Robert F. Allen in his book, *Beat The System*.[1] The key areas Allen lists are: rewards and permissions; modeling behavior; information and communication systems; interactions and relations; training; and allocation of resources.

REWARDS AND PERMISSIONS

Rewards can be anything that people value—money, privileges (parking spaces given for status, longevity, or for getting to work first), benefits (more life insurance for older, higher-paid employees, or chosen by the employee), information (results restricted to key managers or disseminated to everyone), belonging (separate dining rooms for officers and for everyone else). Our chapter on compensation lists rewards other than money and explains how to use them.

The most visible reward is promotion, since promotions are a regular sign of the behavior you want to reward. If you promote people because they are relatives, your personnel manual does not have to mention that nepotism counts. In time, you will lose your strong nonfamily managers. If you promote people for longevity, for not making mistakes since they took no risks, or for agreeing and never arguing, you are making clear the behavior you want.

[1]McGraw-Hill Book Company, 1980.

MODELING BEHAVIOR

The performance, informality, and hours of the top people; the lushness or leanness of the working environment and expenses; whether owners are addressed by their first or last names; and the respect managers have for their subordinates are examples of behavior modeling. As people come into a new culture or organization, they are especially sensitive to the norms. New employees are quickly indoctrinated into the norms applying to hours, production, quality, and even stealing. In some retail organizations, the level of inventory shortages management has tolerated is passed on at the first coffee break.

Managers can use the sensitivity new employees have to the organization by carefully picking the supervisors who will handle orientation. Almost every company has people who represent the behavior you want others to model and who are proud of their teaching ability. New employees should spend their first weeks or months, depending on level, with those employees.

For the same reason, a new high level manager should spend most of his first few weeks with the CEO. If you want expenses to be tight, the top managers must be tight in their expenses. No announcements had to be made of the change in acceptable expense norms when the president of a dental supply firm exchanged fourteen Cadillacs for fourteen Hondas. At the same time, a new CEO should appraise the informal power structure and the ability of the existing organization to tolerate change before she makes major moves.

INFORMATION AND COMMUNICATION SYSTEMS

Who receives information and what kind shows how information is used as a sign of power. People denied information available to others, especially to peers, feel insecure and not trusted.

What is monitored and followed up in regular reports also illustrates what management thinks is important. For example, it is a common credo that "People are our most important asset." It is equally common to see no items dealing with people in the regular weekly or monthly operating or variance reports except as they are shown in units and dollars.

Signs that people count are a newsletter and bulletin board reporting on personal and organizational changes, plans, business goals and results, and new employees with a picture and short biography; an indoctrination program that includes the personal introduction of the new employee to the highest-level manager the size of the company permits; a final screening before employment by the

CEO or top executive; and an ombudsman system whereby an employee can go outside the hierarchy to appeal what he feels is an injustice without worrying that his immediate superior will find out. Note how much more practical these steps are in a small company than in a large one.

If people are important, the communication system can be used to support the policy. If numbers are important, the system will show that priority, in part by the absence of significant communications dealing with people. Managers rarely are aware of the effects of what they do not communicate. They may improve the consistency of the working environment using techniques that show employees what is important.

Do people have all the information they need to do their jobs? In a plant that cured calfskins to be sold to tanners, the foreman of the curing cellar was given minimum information by the owners. As a responsible manager he kept his own records of the inventory levels at each stage in the curing cycle, the prices at which the hides were bought and sold, and the gross margin his operation produced. By denying him the information the owners encouraged an adversary relationship.

A simple solution to the need-to-know question is to ask: what do you need and want to know so that you can do your job better?

The final question you might want to ask to test the norms of information is: Do people communicate with others at all levels, naturally? One of the hard-to-change environmental factors that affects communication is the physical layout of the office or factory. If groups are separated by floors, decor, difficulty in seeing and visiting each other, or by behavioral norms that discourage informal communication, the company is making clear, usually inadvertently, that it does not want people to communicate. If coffee and copying machines are placed so that they bring people together, they will.

In companies where management has decided that communication between groups is to be encouraged, office, parking, eating, meeting, and common spaces are planned so that it is hard for people of different rank and from different groups *not* to talk to each other. A typical example is the high-technology company that placed sales representatives and engineers on the same floor. They shared the same lavatories, office supply sources, eating facilities, entrance, and parking spaces. Top management in that company was making sure that any antagonism which might exist or arise between the two groups had maximal opportunity to be talked about and dealt with. Top management used other measures, such as assigning individuals from each group to work for a week with the other, scheduling weekly meetings between project managers, and tying compensation rewards to the successful development of new jointly developed products, to strengthen joint efforts and to foster understanding.

INTERACTIONS AND RELATIONS

Mr. Allen asks some penetrating questions to identify the norms in this area. Does management take steps to increase interaction through the creation of task forces, problem-solving groups, or brainstorming sessions? Are personnel policies developed to reduce the chance that discrimination will slip in? Is it safe for people at any level to initiate change? In a thirty-store retail clothing chain the father and son who owned the company planned to update the warehouse, a $2 million project. Asked by an outsider what he thought about it, the sixty-two-year-old warehouse manager, who had been with the company over forty years, said that he thought the job could be done for $500,000, but that since he had not been asked his opinion, he certainly was not going to volunteer it. His lifetime experience had proved that all ideas came from the top, and since the top knew how it wanted to spend its money, he was not going to confuse them with his opinion.

How groups refer to each other is a sign of how they relate. Typically, the "we-they" syndrome implies that one group is for the company and the other is against it or at least less committed. When mistakes occur, is the major effort to find the culprit and punish her, or is the mistake first analyzed as a system deviation, rather than an individual's weakness or intention?

Suggestion systems often have a short life because they can demean the group being asked for its suggestions. The systems usually are visible signs that the groups for which they are developed are outside the inner circle. The fact that such systems are not used at the managerial level hints that lower level employees have to be asked or bribed to come up with ideas. The administrative handling of suggestions gives a message about how important the system is. If every suggestion is evaluated and answered within a short time, no more than a week, and proper recognition is given to those adopted, a suggestion system can enhance relationships.

TRAINING

If management thinks that training is important, it will evaluate training programs and ensure that each employee has the training he or she needs. The norms pertaining to training are demonstrated by the commitment and model behavior of top people.

A consulting psychologist was called in by the owner-manager of a chain of department stores to develop a training program for the clerks and buyers whose productivity and customer relationships were below the levels the CEO expected. The psychologist refused to consider the engagement unless the CEO agreed to be the first person to submit to training. The organization's norms of behavior could be improved only if the CEO changed *his* behavior by showing what was important. The first step was to show that he had to be trained. After three days of one-on-one meetings with the psychologist, the CEO proudly announced the new program. Working down the organization to make sure that the norms would be reinforced, the training team changed the standards of acceptable behavior in terms of customer relationships and productivity. After six months, productivity and sales both had risen by more than 12 percent.

ALLOCATION OF RESOURCES

There are simple, obvious norms of resource allocation. Money, space, salary and bonus increases, capital equipment, and research expenditures are examples. But the company's norms also show in the allocation of the top managers' *time*, the largest unrecorded corporate asset. How do they spend their time? What questions do they ask? How do they follow up? How do they get information outside formal channels? What do they want to know? Whom do they target for advancement and then spend time in showing the ropes? Who is introduced to the banker and the major customers, taken on inspection trips, and invited to the CEO's home to be tested for social acceptance?

Is top management still unaware of Peter Drucker's advice of thirty years ago—resources should be devoted to opportunities and taken from problems? A $1-million-a-year dental laboratory servicing dentists within fifty miles of Chicago was barely breaking even. Competition from low-quality laboratories, mail order firms in areas with lower labor costs, and an excess of local laboratory capacity made it difficult to earn a profit. The owner turned down every suggestion of a marketing consultant to increase sales and margins because the owner said he could not afford the money or the time. The suggestions included: (1) spending $2,000 for market research to tell the owner how customers and potential customers ranked him and competitors, (2) the CEO's spending time to identify a niche in the market he could exploit to avoid remaining in a no-win commodity pricing status, and (3) hiring part-time, retired dentists or technicians who could use their contacts and expertise at lower cost and risk than full-time sales representatives could.

Attitude surveys and consultants who are able to listen to employees from different levels in the company are the best identifiers of how people feel. Employees cannot be fooled. They respond to actions, not to words. They are also cautious. They want to know what management's reaction will be so they can act with confidence. The smaller company has the ability to create the atmosphere most likely to bring forth ideas and risk-taking and to change the level of expectations *if* the top managers know what working environment they want and use all the techniques at their disposal to communicate it.

In the face of inconsistency, people are confused, unwilling to change, alienated, defensive, and self-protective. Two examples may help: How free are people about expressing their feelings? Does the company norm accept the show of emotion, or are people supposed to hold in their feelings from nine to five? The boss randomly blows his top, his brother-in-law rants when production is off, and his daughter-in-law brings her marital troubles to the office; but, when someone not in the family expresses his feelings, it is clear from the boss's unspoken reaction that the wrong behavior has been shown. Under these confusing circumstances, employees will be careful not to show any emotion, and thereby deprive management of important guides to decision-making.

A second example is the disclosure of strategic decisions. Spreading the word makes people feel a part of the organization but increases the risk of disclosure. In World War II, an OSS rule of thumb was that confidentiality decreased by the power of the number of informed people: two knowledgeable people meant the chance of keeping the secret was one in four; three people meant one chance in twenty-seven. Keeping strategic decisions secret until they are disclosed through action alienates those who were excluded. The establishment of a balance between the two potentially positive but contradictory positions is a sign that managerial philosophy is not being formed by default.

Open Management

The reality of management-personnel styles is in the evidence of what managements do, not in what they say. Terry Farnsworth's article, "How to Test Your Board," in the October 1981 issue of *Management Today* raises some of the questions employees might ask in response to typical management pronouncements:

> If "people are our most important asset," does the individual worker see himself as an asset? Is he shown that he counts through the

evidence of the fairness of his salary, the quality of his working conditions, and the way he is appraised and rewarded?

If his opportunities are described as "the sky's the limit," does the evidence back the statement, or is the truth that promotions are limited, specific educational and family relationships determine who gets ahead, and the conservatism of the firm's management reduces growth opportunities for everyone?

Are raises, equipment needs, competitive fringes, and salaries denied because "we can't afford it" when the evidence in the income statement and cash flow shows that they can?

Employees accept such treatment for two reasons: they lack the information necessary to rebut the arguments since salary and promotion policies are secretive, and few employees in closely held, smaller companies have ever worked elsewhere and therefore they cannot make comparisons.

As the German and Japanese examples have shown us, workers and manager-owners share the same long-term goals: a healthy, growing business that is attractive and decent to work in. Answering Mr. Farnsworth's last question brings these issues out clearly. "We believe in open management." Everyone in the firm wants to know how it is doing in the market and what its plans are to maintain competitive superiority of products and services in the future. Both the firm's management and the worker should be clear about pay—the firm should know what it needs to get its money's worth, the employee should know what is expected of him.

The way decisions that affect the company and the individual worker are made is a concern of everyone. If the worker has some idea of the standards her bosses are using to make decisions, she may be able to add to the pool of information. She may also be more careful in checking the information she passes on.

How people can progress in the firm is of general interest. The right people are more likely to remain with a firm if they know what's ahead. Even the delicate subject of how profits are to be distributed among shareholders, managers, and other employees might be considered part of an open management policy. Different people will be attracted to a firm depending on whether they find out what's going on by after-the-fact evidence or by announcements that precede the fact.

Employees want to have input into decisions that directly affect them. An open management style allows for that input.

Finally, open management means that workers may question how top management is staying up to date to deal with their common future. What is being done to perpetuate the company and provide the new skills it will need in the future? Consider the effect on a work force of executives, as part of an open management style, announcing their management development program to assure workers that they are trying to prepare for the future. An organization deserving of commitment and support will be tough-minded in its self-evaluation as to discrepancies between what management says and what it does.

The following list summarizes systems and signals to help a smaller company manager develop the internal consistency that will make the environment clear to employees so they will feel more free to express themselves.

1. *Use of time.* How do managers spend their time: reviewing financial statements, checking on the progress of management development, listening or talking, asking questions or knowing answers? Are managers in their offices or in the field, plant, or marketplace? Do managers wait for problems to surface or do they seek out incipient problems?

2. *Questions.* Are questions asked over and over? Persistent, reiterative questioning, getting to the bottom, accepting only facts and a wide variety of opinions shows what is important.

3. *Agendas.* What is covered in formal meetings, informal sessions, and performance evaluation reviews? What is not on the agenda? Items that are rarely covered but whose inclusion hint at a special sort of company are mistakes, variances, superior performance, people development, the outside world, customers' changing needs, competitors' likely strategies, exploiting the company's major strengths, and defending it against its major exposures.

4. *Reports.* What you inspect is what you expect. If reports are voluminous, the implication is that the subordinate is incompetent, because the boss has to check on everything. If reports deal only with key factors and major variances in both directions, the implication is that the boss assumes that the subordinate is keeping her results in line.

   From whose perspective are questions asked and reports generated—internal or external, customers' or owners'?

   What is assumed to be the normal source of problems—the individual (lazy, greedy, and disloyal) or the environment (competition, equipment, training, information, or system)?

   What is the standard of performance—the past, budget goals, competitors, objective measures, or personal traits?

5. *Committees, task forces.* Invitation to membership can be flattering or it can be a way of shutting up dissidents because the task force report is buried or sent back for more data. Are committees used to support the belief in participative decision-making where practical?

6. *Rewards.* Critical because they can motivate, rewards should be used with care to reinforce the behavior and results you want. Spontaneous rewards are especially useful because they can follow immediately after the performance you want to recognize, making clear to everyone what counts.

7. *Settings.* Where and how often does the manager meet with his people—in his office or theirs? Where are planning meetings held and how are they conducted? Are people encouraged to evaluate all meetings so that they can be improved or dropped?

8. *Physical contact between people.* Where and what is headquarters? Is it a founder's memorial or a place that encourages people to circulate easily? Is it easy for departments and individuals to mix?

9. *Informal-formal contact.* Are bosses available only by appointment—so busy they show how unimportant are those trying to see them? "I feel I'm taking Sarah's time away from something more important when, after waiting three weeks to see her, I finally get ten minutes of her time."

10. *Risk-taking.* Does the company kill off disturbing, new ideas with: "We tried that." "No one in the industry does it and we can't afford to be first." "Why change a successful formula?" "We don't ask those types of questions around here." Since people are more interested in protecting their self-images than in increasing corporate profits, they are not going to risk that image if the result of making a suggestion is a squelch. Since many new ideas are directly or indirectly critical of something that is now accepted, it is hard for managers to listen patiently and without emotion to a suggestion that implies that some policy, product, or decision they made is wrong. As long as the manager's reaction hints at resentment, he will remain uncriticized and the organization will lose the contribution. If you want to encourage new ideas, figure out how to test them cheaply and quickly. Initiators should have access to many potential approvers. Wide dissemination increases the possibility of support. Reward risk-taking that failed, if the decision to take the risk was reached rationally with all the information then available.

11. *A few closely watched numbers or monitors that support key people.* Top managers give direction and support and also freedom to their proteges. The support and the freedom are signs of style and direction.

12. *Deliberate attempt to find problems.* Top managers should spend time seeking out and investigating the variances (plus and minus), the glitches, and bottlenecks to find the reasons for broad changes. Examples of a desire to innovate, challenge, and get to the bottom are:

    Managers check out returns, allowances, lawsuits, lost customers, and declining or increasing service-product trends.

    They interview and listen to outstanding young managers before any problems arise about their careers.

    They handle exit interviews of good people who leave.

    They ask customers how the company can improve its service and then act on the findings.

13. *Precise, measurable, achievable, stretching, and short-term milestones, the next milestone set only after the previous one has been reached.* Long-range plans may be dangerous unless you regularly challenge the assumptions behind them. Short-term achievements lend credibility to change. They encourage striking out in new directions with a minimum of confusion in changing targets. Insistence on *measurable* results highlights a basic performance improvement rule: People work best when they know specifically what they are expected to do and by when. Different plans, reports, controls, and rewards are needed for the changing, new, growth parts of the business (e.g., product, personnel policy, compensation program, hiring, training, advertising) and for the established, known, maintenance, repetitive areas.

14. *Concern for facts, a skeptical challenge of information sources.* Franklin D. Roosevelt is reported to have given the same secret assignment to two or three trusted aides to make sure that he got unbiased opinions. Dr. Glenn Bassett says that the bases of every major decision should be second-sourced. Do not commit the company or make a hard-to-change move without having at least two independent opinions. Do not invest in or get rid of a business, segment, product line, branch, or professional relationship until you have checked with two independent sources. And do not hire, promote, fire a key person, or change a personnel policy unless you have done the same.

Second-sourcing implies rational decision-making, which is an element of a consistent environment.

15. *Results.* Ideas are cheap and readily available. Successful companies do an extraordinary job in implementation. What the manager asks about *after* a plan or decision has been agreed to and how she overcomes difficulties show whether the issue matters. For example: if people count, short, weekly, monthly, and then quarterly reviews with a new employee show management's concern.

16. *Objective review of reasons for failures and successes.* If done as joint learning, without recrimination or win-lose situations, the review can support risk-taking. Done with finger-pointing, the review kills initiative and is divisive and protective.

17. *Positive reinforcement in a public setting.* B. F. Skinner was right when he urged quick, clear reinforcement of desired behavior. There should be no doubt about why a reward is being given. Consider the effect of recognizing a good idea submitted by someone low in the organization by having him present it to his peers, superiors, or the company's board of directors.

Internal consistency in itself is not necessarily useful. It serves the organization only when it supports objectives. As Bruce Henderson[2] has written, "Objectives make possible the creation and productivity of an organization. Objectives determine the membership . . . the rank and status of an organization's members. Objectives determine who can take initiative and the leadership in an organization." Without objectives, people end up serving themselves, not because they are necessarily selfish, but because in a vacuum of organizational objectives they have no choice.

Few organizations offer membership benefits intrinsically equal to the sacrifice involved or required. People stay in a firm for the psychological value of membership—the respect, achievement, and feeling of being part of an organization which is in itself respected, admired, and valued by the society of which it is a part. The objectives, therefore, determine the lifestyle, the value system, the membership, and the culture.

No one will stay in or give more than lip service to an organization without believing it is acting in his best interest. Valued objectives are not petty, mean, or of use only to a few. They go beyond the present and the individual.

[2]*Objectives and the Organization*, Boston Consulting Group, 1981.

Before you start changing your organization, be sure of what you want to change *to*. Group objectives should be sufficiently strong to overcome personal needs and objectives. Henderson concludes that strategy (norm) development is a waste without worthwhile objectives and commitment to them. In summary:

1. Decide what atmosphere, culture, or norms you now have. Use attitude surveys, listening, or consultants.

2. Decide what your market uniqueness, strategy, objectives, and competitive plus are to be. Try to list your own values as they relate to who should make decisions, have information, and share rewards.

3. Define the gap between the culture you have and the one you want.

4. With the participation of those involved, apply all the management systems and techniques to get the message through clearly and consistently. It will take one or two years of sending consistent messages in the smaller company before people will accept the new environment. Since people can keep in focus, and management can only concentrate on, a few key factors, select the goals and standards critical to your strategy, and then orchestrate them with every imaginative technique you can think of.

Personnel Policies and Trust

Personnel or human resources strategies swing between warm, paternal-fraternal do-goodism and practical applications of motivational findings that support a manager's value system. Do-goodism is blind to economic, organizational, and psychological realities. A third possibility is tough, insensitive, autocratic demands based on fear. Such hardheadedness is often effective in the short run. Being tough satisfies power needs and usually improves the current income statement. But it is as out of touch with the realities of working environments as is the philosophy that everyone should like everyone and workers should be as interested in the company's success as its owners and managers are.

We would summarize our approach to human resources management with one word: trust. What workers suspect of management and what management is willing to disclose and share with workers generally are functions of trust. In one-on-one relationships between superior and subordinate, the trust level is the determining factor in the success of management by objectives, performance appraisals, disciplinary action, criticism, and management development. Since trust takes time to develop, there are no simple ways to develop it. In companies of two hundred or fewer people, it usually takes a minimum of two years before top management actions are accepted as consistently dependable and workers and second-level managers feel comfortable exposing their security and self-image to more risk-taking.

Individual relationships can be changed in a shorter period. The length of time taken and degree of change depend almost entirely on the boss. We have all met people who gave us a feeling of trustworthiness in the first few minutes or hours spent with them. If they demonstrate in some manner that they feel *we* are trustworthy, we are likely to show more of ourselves. Someone who admits ignorance, requests help, discloses information, actively listens, and shares recognition and rewards makes us feel more comfortable. If our trust is not violated or exploited, we gradually drop our reserve and the relationship is strengthened.

We call people who offer their trust and are taken advantage of naive. Lending money to strangers who disappear, giving information that is misused, asking for help and then finding it is not forthcoming, or offering hospitality that is abused are typical examples of the learning experiences young people go through which build skepticism and suspicion. In a working environment most people protect themselves and take few risks being hurt by misplaced trust.

Creativity and Innovation

Perhaps the strongest attraction between an employee and an organization is generated when the employee can contribute new ideas and have them evaluated outside the bonds of habit and history. Our observation is that where creativity is valued one finds the most competent and content employees.

A common complaint of owner-managers of smaller companies is that they are the only ones interested in the company: no one else has ideas, no one else cares. We could legitimately inquire of the complainers: whatever happened to the innovative, creative, loyal employee who in the early days took the firm's survival and success as seriously as the owner did? The chances are the answer would be: they're still here, but they've changed. We would not often accept such answers. Experience leads us to believe the old employees are still there, unchanged. What has changed is the organizational climate.

The assumptions about human nature underlying all personnel management attitudes and programs include some about creativity: that creativity is rare or common, that it is native or can be taught, and the like. We feel that creativity is primarily a function of a company's climate. With that conviction, we list several techniques to improve creativity.

It is not universally accepted that creativity is a top criterion in choosing a top executive. Only about one-seventh of the CEOs in a recent study[3] felt that creativity was an important qualification for top management selection. Perhaps one reason is that creative people are seen as being either crazy or mystical, characteristics generally regarded as incompatible with organizational life.

To us, creativity is a precondition for corporate survival and growth; is far more common than most of us think; and is vastly undervalued and underused. We say it is a precondition because it is one of the sources of uniqueness—that key to corporate health and longevity.

Creativity is more common than we are inclined to think because it is as much a feature of working brains as remembering, calculating, and reasoning are. In fact, it is inseparable from them. What makes it rare in business is that businesspeople prefer order, process, and predictability to the new, discontinuous, and venturous—despite the obviousness of the fact that the most successful firms are that because they have made practical use of creativity.

One way of stimulating innovation is to separate areas of certainty and uncertainty. Since most results are evaluated in terms of the bottom line, the accounting reporting system gives primacy to the certainties of the business. Taking risks, making mistakes, being creative just for the fun of it or to extend the firm's horizons in products, services, or personnel practices are overshadowed by the certainties, receive no recognition in the financial statements, and have practically no chance of tolerance in the typical firm.

An example was the $7 million fifty-year-old service organization with three offices on the East Coast that had a chance to buy a small related business in one of the British Virgin Islands for $25,000, payable over three years. The deal was rejected by the majority of the principals not because of price, terms, or risk, but because it had little opportunity for growth, would be hard to supervise, and no one wanted to live permanently on the relatively unsophisticated tropical island. The person who proposed the acquisition agreed that the objections were valid, but felt they could be overcome: the purchase was not for growth but for fun; the level of work was so simple

[3]Reported in *Issues & Observations*. Greensboro, N.C.: Center for Creative Leadership, November 1981.

that minimum supervision was needed; and one of the purposes in the deal was to have young members of the firm spend two months a year on the island. Mainly, the deal was proposed to introduce some sparkle and sizzle into a firm that had symptoms of organizational arteriosclerosis.

Some suggestions to increase creativity are:

1. Consider giving employees sabbaticals. Sabbaticals have been part of the academic fringe benefit package for years. In the smaller company, they offer an alternative to "burnout" and the opportunity to think, rarely available in sufficient doses to operating executives.

2. Send people away from the office to solve the problem. A division of a consumer product company developed a series of new products based on an old successful one by putting a group of eight engineers and marketing people, who had been unable to resolve their differences, together in a hotel room on Friday and telling them they should not come back to their regular jobs until they came up with answers satisfactory to both groups. Under the leadership of the divisional vice-president, they emerged Sunday evening with a campaign that tripled the division's sales and profits within a year. This was an effective, if hot-house, treatment.

3. Trade people with similar but noncompeting firms. Trading people is common in the army, church, and nonprofit sector. It is available to smaller companies willing to make the effort. Professional athletes may ask to be traded not because they want more money, but because they want to play in new and more challenging situations. Smaller company managers have the same need.

4. Seek variety in solutions by starting at the bottom of the organizational chart. It is an old but still effective tactic to ask the youngest member for her ideas about a problem first. Not knowing what her superiors have in mind, she has to come up with her own best ideas—an excellent source of novelty and variety.

5. Encourage the contribution of the irrational, unconscious in problem-solving. Since solutions develop best from a relevant data base, first collect the information needed, then allow an incubation period long enough for creativity to have a chance. The luxury of time is rare—so is creativity.

6. Strengthen the organizational effects of innovation by taking the full burden of absorbing them from the innovator. In some

companies, creative ideas have partners: one who suggests, does the work, and accepts the risk; and one who blocks for him and smooths the organizational snags and bumps.

7. Encourage innovation throughout the organization. Give recognition for challenging the past and for asking "why." Question all policies and procedures at least every three years.

Reducing Problems of Change

Managers have perceived employees to be resistant to change and that resistance to be a constraint to making progress. The view is one-sided and destructive. Change is as much needed as it is likely to engender resistance. Only impaired human beings prefer a changeless environment. The best employees, those interested in the firm's and their own prosperity, welcome and facilitate change. Therefore, managers should devote far more time to identifying and implementing productive changes than to figuring out how to overcome resistance to change.

Still, changes must be made carefully. In any situation, a change should be introduced so as to give it the best chance for survival with the least damage to morale and efficiency. Some guidelines to achieving that objective are:

1. Make certain the change is necessary. Change for the sake of change alone is always damaging, both to morale and efficiency. The only changes that avoid such damage are those that are recognized by those affected as benefiting them and the organization, probably in that order.

2. Involve personnel in appraising the value of the change and determining how best to introduce it. It does not matter how or from what sources the idea sprang. Few employees view themselves as change agents, having accepted early in their business careers the hierarchical nature of the power structure. But they also believe *they* know best how to do the work they are involved in; and changes imposed upon them are most likely to be resented and, therefore, resisted. Before declaring the changes, involve the affected people in determining their value, their nature, and how and when to implement them. Involvement has two benefits:

Involved people are more likely than anyone to find whatever flaws there are in the proposed changes.

They are more likely to feel positively about the changes after having had a hand in shaping them than if the changes are imposed by higher authority.

3. Pick an acceptable leader to make the change. Changes cannot be made effectively by committee. The responsibility for introducing and seeing the change through its first days should always be given to one person. And no change, however valuable, can survive a leader who is unacceptable to those affected by the change.

Bringing Employees into the Action

We have discussed techniques to improve relations between top management and employees and to make better use of human resources; but none of them can be fully effective without knowledge of how employees feel about the company, their pay, their prospects, the future, products, and the like. Most companies know little about the things that govern employees' behavior. Thus, the firm that intends to employ its human resources fully takes pains to find out how employees feel. We have found formal attitude surveys to be most satisfactory for this purpose.

One of the common assumptions of smaller company managers is that their size and informal personal relations permit them to cut through organizational fog well enough that they really know how their employees feel. Personnel decisions are then made on the basis of what the manager thinks his people feel or want.

Unfortunately, smaller size does not automatically guarantee upward communication of feelings and ideas. Self-preservation of image, status, security, and peace on the job has a higher priority for most employees than does a desire to help the company by providing input to improve decisions. Although the number of organizational levels is fewer in smaller firms than in larger firms, the number of levels is less a factor in communication than is the thickness of the psychological barrier between any manager and his subordinates. Because smaller organizations are more easily dominated by a single strong manager, they are *more*, not less, likely to have clogged communication.

We have asked hundreds of individuals and groups in smaller companies how things could be done better, in any way. After getting the answers we asked, "What did management say of your idea?" and the second answers really pointed out the only common answer: "We didn't tell the boss." Almost invariably, the reason given for not telling was that no one ever asked previously. "Why didn't you just walk in and tell the boss what you thought? The idea is good and he would appreciate it." Our respondents usually answer that someone once suggested a change and was led to believe, directly or otherwise, that her job was to follow orders, not come up with ideas; or she was told the suggestion dealt with something that was on the secret agenda of subjects not to be questioned.

For example, the CEO of a successful contracting firm was set against pensions because he believed employees should provide for their own retirement out of their above-average base and bonus pay. He also resented the government's intrusion into his business through Social Security deductions and taxes. Finally, to support his opposition to pensions, he said that he had surveyed employees five years before for their preference between a pension or a 7 percent raise, and the employees had overwhelmingly chosen the raise.

The facts that the employees were now older, that the company was stronger, and that the acceptance of pensions was more widespread did not concern him. He said he knew his people and was on a first-name basis with at least half of the three hundred employees and that in the previous five years no one had come through his door to tell him he wanted a pension plan.

The distortion of reality is almost farcical. Consultants suggested he repeat the employee survey. This time, the responses showed that 85 percent of the employees preferred the pension to an automatic raise.

USING SURVEYS

The example leads us to the conclusion that attitude or employee morale surveys are an inexpensive and valuable personnel tool. Since morale is both a cause and a result of other environmental conditions, it is critical that the smaller company manager get facts and feelings, which are most accurately revealed in surveys. Several surveys are included in the appendix. The one you use depends on the level of education and sophistication of the group being surveyed. Other survey forms are available from personnel consultants or from organizations that specialize in developing them.

Writing survey questions is not a job for amateurs. The choice of words can be critical. Each question must aim at getting feelings or facts on only one subject and should offer a range of answers. The questionnaire should have internal checks: questions dealing with an important subject should be asked several different ways. The questions must be simple, clear, and consistent, and yield answers of similar quality.

If you do not engage a consultant to help choose or design a survey, pick one form and use it in its entirety. Generally, to maintain integrity, it is safer to drop than to add questions. If you want to cover a specific subject that is not part of a form you otherwise like, ask someone with survey design experience to edit your additional questions to make sure they hit the target.

Generally, we suggest that questionnaires be filled out anonymously. Until employees feel comfortable with the use of the survey information and are confident that they do not have to worry about the consequences of saying how they feel, they will be careful in what they say and to whom. Anonymity removes most of those fears.

Experience has shown, to the chagrin of some owner-managers, the level of employee distrust. In one such case, the survey form was enclosed in the Friday payroll envelope with instructions to complete it anonymously and deposit it in a ballot-like box on Monday morning. Of one hundred and fifty forms distributed, only twenty-five responses were turned in. The employees suspected, without foundation, that their individual surveys had been secretly identified with a magic ink and that their anonymity would be compromised. After a decent interval, the company tried again. This time the blank forms were left on a table and people were asked to pick one as they left the plant on Friday afternoon. With the guarantee of anonymity, almost everyone responded.

In addition to guaranteeing anonymity, make sure that the memo accompanying the survey explains that management is distributing it to find out how to improve the company. Make it clear that management will do whatever it can that is suggested. If you cannot act, explain why.

A basic rule in using attitude surveys is not to start unless you are prepared to finish. The mere distribution of a survey commits you, at a minimum, to some feedback. You cannot respond to a survey form by excusing or explaining your way out of all employee requests. Be prepared to act. Asking people what they think implies you are going to listen with an open mind and that, if the suggestions are reasonable, you will do something about them.

The way survey suggestions are used can strengthen the relationship between superiors and subordinates. Rensis Likert's linking-pin concept suggests that your influence over subordinates is increased to the extent that they can influence *your* decisions. Rather than reducing supervisory power, responding to survey suggestions probably increases it.

Attitude surveys imply a partnership. Employees will tell management how they feel and what they think can be done to improve the company; management will summarize what was said; and change will follow. Feedback to survey participants softens the we-they relationship.

You can handle feedback in several ways.

1. Calculate the percentages for each response and distribute a completed survey form with the answers you received. Comment on how you intend to handle sensitive or critical areas. This approach is open, clean, and immediately establishes management's intent to work with employees on common problems.
2. Pick out the key items, both positive and negative, and summarize the results with editorial comments. Because employees are more likely to suspect a doctoring of responses and selective disclosure of embarrassing subjects, this approach is less forthright but is still useful, particularly as a first step.
3. Report the results in either of the above ways and then ask for volunteers to look into ways of solving major problem areas. This policy moves the survey from an information-gathering technique to an action plan. It is the most successful approach, since it defuses the critics, brings employees into fact-gathering and consulting, and usually produces fast and practical answers to problems.

A smaller company does not move from an autocratic to a consultative management style merely by using attitude surveys. A manager has to overcome a large hurdle before he can accept the idea that the people he has been telling what to do now know enough so that he should listen to their ideas and even act on them.

Attitude surveys are especially useful to track the effects of organizational and personnel policy changes. Examples of questions that may show whether personnel policies are effective are:

The fairness of pay and fringe benefits

The changing norms of openness and acceptance of suggestions

The use and clarity of performance appraisals

The odds that the individual will be working for the company three or five years from now

The opportunities to grow and to use skills

The relationship between what was promised and delivered in describing a job to an applicant

Some companies find it useful to track responses to attitude surveys over periods, measuring change and seeing where they may have to bring new techniques to bear.

Attitude surveys can also be used in emergency situations. In a multi-plant, non-union company, the CEO learned that a local union had made overtures to workers, who were responsive because of their unhappiness over a variety of working and salary conditions. A survey was created by picking twelve questions from a questionnaire designed for relatively uneducated workers and was distributed the day following the union's overt move. Management requested comments from employees and urged anonymity by suggesting they use a typewriter or ask relatives to write suggestions to disguise the origins of the comments. The memo accompanying the form acknowledged that management was aware of unhappiness and wanted to know the things that most bothered workers. The plant supervisor, who was sensitive enough to admit that he was one of the causes of the unhappiness, had agreed that personal interviews were unlikely to get the truth.

The survey forms were returned filled with vitriolic and pointed criticism. The next day management changed those things that could be done immediately and promised answers on the others within three days. The promise was satisfied and the unionization threat was put aside for the while.

SOURCES

"Corporate Culture." *Business Week*, October 27, 1980

Thomas J. Peters, "Management Systems: The Language of Organizational Character and Competence," *Organizational Dynamics*, Summer, 1980, (New York: AMACOM, a division of American Management Associations, 1980).

Kim Cameron, "Critical Questions in Assessing Organizational Effectiveness," *Organizational Dynamics*, Autumn, 1980, (New York: AMACOM, a division of American Management Associations, 1980).

3 ❦
Determining Staffing Needs

One of the finest services of personnel management is active participation in reassignment and recruiting decisions. Until recently, those decisions were made and implemented in most companies on a segregated, multiple-office basis. Traditionally, deciding the number and kinds of employees needed has been the responsibility of operating managers and/or industrial engineers. To recruit and hire employees was personnel's job in companies large enough to have personnel offices. But that was a defective way of handling staffing.

The problem with the traditional approach is that no one sees the personnel picture in its entirety or closely enough to make the best use of the firm's human resources. Middle managers do not see the firm as a whole, top managers do not see it in sufficient detail. As a result, the traditional, segmented approach to staffing is being replaced by a holistic approach, combining particular with overall needs, and intensive knowledge of both with knowledge of internal and external resources. The approach has expanded the personnel function far beyond its original borders.

In the most profitable larger firms, personnel has a big part in deciding who gets promoted, reassigned, discharged, and hired. It brings to the staffing process the skills and knowledge that unite the formerly separated elements. Smaller firms follow the traditional approach in most cases, primarily because they do not have personnel departments or a single personnel manager. They would benefit from adopting a holistic approach to staffing decisions.

If a single personnel management seems unrealistic, look at the time and money you spend in recruiting people, training them, and coping with employees promoted beyond their capacities. These costs are greater than most of the indirect costs of business.

Closing the Organizational Gap

Although keeping the enterprise "lean and mean" is accepted as an article of faith by managers, not many of them manage in accordance with the article. While usually aggressive in their searches for objective means for controlling purchasing, inventories, production, accounts payable, and other operations, managers are likely to be quite the opposite when it comes to controlling the size and complexity of the organization.

Hiring, for example, is customarily based on filling vacancies as they occur in outdated organizational structures or on filling positions created out of subjective interpretations of growth needs. One result is a widening gap between two aggregate staffs, one with enough people to do the work needed to achieve the results wanted and no more, and one with enough people to do what has been added beyond the essential work as well. It is amazing how much unessential work can be hung onto the essential.

Because organizational obesity is so common, the first responsibility of the personnel function is to see the firm's human resources, from top to bottom, for what they are; in other words, to take and keep a perpetual human resource inventory. To know the value of the inventory, the appropriateness of its makeup, and its availability, personnel needs to know what the firm's goals are. With that knowledge in hand, it can take the next step of determining the firm's work and skill needs and keeping them in balance. That step, which appears to trespass upon industrial engineering's territory, is an essential part of an effective personnel function.

Organizational structure, important as it is, is usually a consequence of non-organizational decisions. The logic of institutional decision-making calls for making decisions about structure after operating and planned needs are decided. Therefore, the quality of organizational structure is never better than the quality of planning and operating decisions.

Because the quality of planning and operating decisions ranges from bad to excellent and the majority of decisions are mediocre, the organizational needs of the enterprise are usually misconceived and people are sometimes reassigned or recruited for jobs which contribute little to the enterprise and are, therefore, unsatisfying. As a result, organizational and staffing decisions should always be traced back to their origins. The underlying decisions should be checked out, and additional factfinding and analysis should be done in the cases of inadequately supported decisions.

Unless the business is correctly understood and plans for it are correctly laid, the work to be done cannot be correctly described and organized. Achieving such understanding marks the beginning of good personnel management. The size of the company is irrelevant; all companies that want to prosper must have it!

Interpreting Turnover

Turnover statistics are a key to effective personnel managment,[1] but they have to be read with care. Concern should be not only with the raw numbers, but also with the quality of people who stay and who leave.

Turnover is calculated by taking the total number of people at the beginning and end of a period, averaging the numbers and dividing the average into the total number of people who worked in the company or department for the period minus the average. The result multiplied by one hundred is the turnover rate.

For a company, the number of W-2 forms issued at the end of the year would be a proper numerator. Say you had one hundred and fifty W-2 forms and one hundred people were on the payroll at the beginning and end of the year. Your turnover ratio as calculated in the equations below is 50 percent.

$$\frac{100 + 100}{2} = 100$$

$$\frac{150 - 100}{100} \times 100 = .5 \times 100 = 50$$

If you lost fifty marginal people and replaced them with above-average workers, the statistic is healthy. If you lost fifty above-average

[1]Obviously, the observation only applies to companies with sufficient turnover.

people and replaced them with average performers, the statistic is unhealthy.

Compare turnover statistics to a haircut. We measure the skill of the barber more by the hair he leaves on the head than on the floor. In an advertising agency, the 50 percent mentioned above reveals a real problem: the turnover of 300 percent in one department headed by a disturbed supervisor. Replacing the supervisor caused the company turnover rate to drop to an industry average figure of 15 percent.

Cost of turnover can be computed for any company in terms hard enough to be accepted by everyone. Include the following:

1. Out-of-pocket costs in the form of costs of advertising, fees to personnel agencies or executive search firms, travel and living expenses for interviewers who had to travel to conduct interviews, and expense reimbursements for candidates who had to travel to be interviewed

2. Salary costs of those recruiting and indoctrinating, interviewing, reference-checking, and training

3. Salary costs covering the indoctrination and training of those recruited

4. The difference in output between what an experienced employee would produce and the new employee will produce[2]

5. The time of other workers, subordinates in the case of a manager, who have to teach the new person her job. This amount is harder to determine, but it is a real cost that shows up in reduced productivity and quality.

To the costs listed must be added the morale effect of turnover: "What's going on around here that causes the good people to leave?" If turnover is caused mainly by firing, and it is not clear why people are being terminated and how far the reduction will go, the effect is normally a drawing-in, self-protective reaction that reduces risk-taking and suggestions for change or improvement.

If it is true that people perform better when they are held ac-

[2]The difference can be determined with fair accuracy when you know what to expect from people at different levels of skill. At a low level, for example, a machine operator or clerical worker might have an acceptable standard of production of one hundred units a day. If the new person produced a daily average of sixty units until he reached standard (say five weeks), and his salary was $300 a week (including all fringes), then one of the costs of turnover would be the difference: 40 percent for learning times $300, or $120 a week times five weeks, or $600.

countable, then applying dollar amounts to turnover may motivate managers to employ their subordinates as assets. For example, when billings dropped in a professional service organization, the top managers differed over whether to drop ten people from the staff. The issue was decided when one of the managers who had done a simple analysis of the cost of hiring a new engineer showed the others it would be $12,000 and that the cost of keeping the ten known, tested people was less than $120,000. Since the firm expected the falloff in business to be temporary, certainly less than a year, the staff was kept intact.

Designing and Describing the Job

The best single control over organizational size, turnover among key employees, and productivity is job design. Smaller companies have generally left the design to natural dynamics: the personalities of job incumbents, individual competences and needs, and top management values and styles. On the whole, that procedure has worked fairly well. But smaller firms can do better by connecting job design more closely to overall planning and subjecting it to formal processes.

The rate of change in an organization lags well behind the changes in its environment, the growth of external opportunities and demands. Job content and organization in smaller companies change only when forces on them become so great that content and relationships crack under the strain. A direct result is that opportunities are missed, achievers become frustrated, and comfort replaces challenge as a motivator.

To introduce an appropriate dynamism in job content and organization, formalize a review process that looks at jobs, organization, and tenure every two years. If done with candor, patience, and some fact-finding, the review process can be rewarding. We have never seen it fail to turn up unnecessary, misplaced, or new, needed work. A review starts with an examination of job descriptions or the writing of them where they are lacking.

One of the most exhaustively studied and talked-about elements in the personnel function is the job description. Countless articles, books, manuals, and seminars tell you how to describe a job, although job descriptions do not have much influence upon individual or organizational performance. We have written thousands of job descriptions but have never seen them used to any extent or make much of a difference.

We believe job descriptions are needed, but not to the extent that has become a habit in industry. Most of the descriptions are not worth the enormous effort put into them and deserve the fate most of them suffer—being stuck away in desk drawers. If a company knows what it wants to accomplish, it does not have to list the responsibilities and authorities of the positions involved. It is sufficient to list the *results* wanted, leaving the how-to to the job incumbent.

Two well-accepted points support our position:

Managers should not be constrained beyond corporate necessities in what they are allowed to do.

Job descriptions are of little use below managerial level jobs.

Managers should be allowed to exercise their ingenuity and innovativeness in making decisions and administering their areas of responsibility. Conventional job descriptions tend to limit those flexibilities. And routine jobs, those with highly repetitive content, have little need for written descriptions.

Not stating the results expected of managerial jobs opens the door to many conflicts, none of which are necessary or productive. The waste involved in resolving them can be totally avoided by a document that specifies the results wanted and, possibly, such matters as the rewards for exceeding them. Finally, the document is essential to evaluating performance. Not having a record of what constitutes standard performance makes it impossible to determine superior performance and reward it equitably.

Answers to the following questions give the job description its substance:

What are the results you need, in as measurable terms as possible? For example, all sales managers do not have the same responsibilities.

Do you want sales maintained, increased (where, with whom—old or new accounts, products, areas) or curtailed because you have decided that selectively reduced sales will increase profits?

Does your product require concern for quality or, because of demand, is quality secondary to delivery?

Do you have a group of sensitive, independent professionals to supervise or a group of less skilled, less demanding workers who need different handling? Acceptable turnover statistics will be completely different in the two cases.

Do you want new products developed as variations of old ones or copied from competitors or to be totally fresh contributions? Again, different results require different people.

The Value of Experience

In making personnel decisions, particularly reassignment and re-cruitment decisions, experience is usually given heavy weight. We think it usually is given too much! To us, experience is invaluable as know-how and as a tool for the creative mind, but it is suffocating as endless repetition and routine. It does not qualify in most circum-stances as the most important criterion for personnel selection, whether reassignment or recruitment.

Dr. Glenn Bassett, a consulting psychologist from Trumbull, Con-necticut, takes a similar view. Based on his work in General Electric Company and with smaller companies as well, Dr. Bassett concluded that we exaggerate the value of experience in determining the num-ber of years it takes to learn a job. One reason for the exaggeration is that we rarely have objective standards or measures of how long it takes people to learn something. For example, the purposes and results of training are seldom evaluated.

The emphasis on experience is particularly high in smaller com-panies. Instead of using linked learning experiences to build career paths and enhance promotability, managers in smaller companies are likely to specify a number of years. To become a sales manager takes three years of field experience; to become a plant superintendent takes at least ten years in our or similar plants; no one can represent this company to the banks, the union, its major customers, or sup-pliers until he is forty years old.

The obsession with years of experience would not be particularly damaging if it did not often result in hiring or promoting those who are more patient than gifted. The gifted candidate usually cannot abide hanging around long enough to experience many times over what she already has learned.

If we go back in history and check the ages of Alexander (who became king at twenty and died, having succeeded reasonably well, at thirty-three), New England sea captains of the China-trade-clipper era (who in their twenties would spend two years in the Far East selling and buying cargoes), and the geniuses of all cultures (many of whom produced their best work early in their careers), we may find reason to question how many years are necessary to learn a position or become qualified for succeeding positions. Dr. Bassett observed that for almost all jobs the incumbent learned 80 percent of what it could teach him in two to five years, and in the same period he brought to the job 80 percent of what he was likely to contribute.

The implications of Bassett's observation are significant: compe-tent managers in any but the fastest changing companies and the rarest jobs, which usually are more titles than assemblages of duties, are likely to run out of new experiences and challenges after a few years on the job. They will be able to handle 80 percent or more of the repetitive problems that come to them without thinking, largely by trained response. True, if they are ambitious, they will test the territorial limits of their job or, if high enough in the company, expand the job to cover new areas. But these efforts, while increasing or maintaining their efficiency, can cause more problems than the benefits they may create. Managers seeking to escape boredom can scarcely escape encroaching on others' territories and defenses. A restless executive in a smaller company can cause all kinds of disturbance through losses in productivity.

The two owners of a $2 million electronic components company called in a consultant to help them investigate an acquisition in which they said they were interested. A superficial examination showed that the deal was a poor one. After looking at eight other potential acquisitions, all of which were turned down for various reasons, and two offers from larger companies who were potential buyers of the electronics firm, the consultant finally realized that the owners had no interest in buying *or* selling. Fifteen years of running the company and achieving levels of earnings and security that satisfied their modest ambition and greed had caused them to turn to buying companies or selling theirs as a pleasant diversion from the all too familiar work of running the company. But they were so secure in their situation that they would not succumb to an attractive deal one way or the other.

A mechanical contracting firm with sales of about $15 million lost the twenty-seven-year-old project manager who had the greatest potential as an owner-manager successor to the three middle-aged owners. After six years with the company, he looked ahead and could see no change in his status or professional growth until the retirement of his immediate boss, one of the owners. That would be at least ten years away, so he quit. He said that he liked the company, respected two of the three owners, but could not wait ten years. He also wanted to learn how other companies handled things since he had seen only one company's viewpoint. He said he might return to the company for a top management job. But, if his new employers turn out to be more sensitive than the first group, they will make sure that the young tiger is kept so busy and challenged being rotated through the organization that his first employers will never see him again.

The smaller firm is not obligated to use years of experience as the principal measure by which it makes its personnel decisions. It can fashion career and experience paths for its key, potential managers or technicians on an individual basis. That is little more time-consuming than researching work records to verify years of experience. Work backward from a definition of the results the company expects from each job. Identify the knowledge and skills that seem to be generally required to produce the results. Do not limit the knowledge and skills to those of the people now in positions responsible for or in support of the achievement of the results; everyone has a different capacity to absorb experience and to generalize from a few experiences. Some people can do something two or three times, see the general application, and do it as well as or better than they shall after doing it a hundred times more. Others take longer to learn to do things.

Fast learning often takes place through a combination of theoretical and factual knowledge and on the job work. Examples are accountants, dentists, teachers, social workers, engineers, jewelers, draftsmen, computer programmers, and forestry experts. Progress in learning these professions can be accelerated by putting together someone who possesses basic technical knowledge or skills with a knowledgeable person capable of passing on what she has learned through on-the-job work.

Experience can be defined as the knowledge needed to move on to the next level or the knowledge needed so that the experts cannot fool you, even inadvertently and without malice. At higher levels in a company, experience includes exposure to the key elements of the business, which permits a manager to make integrated decisions. A CEO who has reached her position primarily through sales, financing, or production has to know enough about the other functions so that she can make balanced corporate decisions. She is more likely to have that balance if she has spent time in the other areas.

The CEO need not know more than anyone about any one specialty, only enough so that she can gauge the bias of a finance, sales, or production manager who provides input to a company-wide decision.

It is also helpful to have enough experience to be sensitive to the problems and outlook of others. A financial manager who has spent a week on the road with a traveling sales representative will hesitate before requesting sales representatives to complete still another form, and will, perhaps, be more gentle in questioning expense reports. The production manager who has joined a sales representative on customer calls may be more sensitive in introducing new products or service procedures. The head of one division of a telephone company required each manager to spend a half day each week on the job with his subordinates. The managers who followed the policy found that the half days provided valuable insight into the attitudes, problems, and expectations of their subordinates. The job visits also opened communication channels, introduced the manager to candidates for advancement, and showed interest in subordinates.

There are other implications of the two to five year limit on a job beyond the perils of boredom. One is the question of what the company gets from its investment in employees' experience. The question regularly arises in salary discussions with employees who have held a job for several years. Their view is that their experience has made them more valuable to the company and, therefore, they should get more money. Put to the challenge of justifying the dollar value of last year's experience, most employees uncomfortably throw the question back by suggesting that their bosses are in the best position to make that evaluation.

When a request for a salary increase for more time on the job is coldly measured against the economic value of time, doubt enters the picture. In some professions, hardheaded managers apply a *negative* factor to increasing years. They have observed that if he has been successful using the skills and knowledge with which he started in his field, he may find it unnecessary and difficult to continue his professional education and stay current. Increasing years may mean outdated professionalism. That most professions require evidence of continuing education is proof of the need. New theories and facts can be catalogued and evaluated. The same cannot be said of additional years on the job.

Coping with Boredom

Faced with minimal opportunities for new experiences because of slow or no growth, the smaller company CEO has several alternatives.

First, she can be selective in personnel choices so that she has no more people than she can accommodate when, after they have derived the 80 percent experience benefit from a position, they want more out of their work. Too much competence is as hard to handle as too little. Identify the few jobs that are critical to corporate success and lure gifted people to fill them. Fill other jobs with people whose capabilities match the jobs and not much else. If you bring in too many gifted people you will soon start losing them, because they will stay with you only as long as they benefit from the experience you offer and soon you will not have anything to offer.

Second, when signs of boredom, diversionary activities, or the development of substantial outside interests appear, he can rotate the person into jobs sufficiently different that learning has to start again. True, there is a core of technical knowledge required in areas such as accounting, factory production, engineering, and personnel. But many cases have proved that people with twenty years in a single or technical discipline are capable of quickly adjusting and contributing to new areas. Once they know enough to understand what they do not know, and if they are confident enough to ask questions, they can apply a fresh look to the critical, strategic elements of the new job.

The best marketing manager an engineering design firm ever had was its former chief designer, who enjoyed dealing with customers' problems more than supervising twelve designers. Turned loose as marketing manager to develop a three-year plan for the firm, he produced an exciting, stretching program that permitted the firm to exploit its skills in inexpensive industrial energy controls.

A personnel manager who created new performance measures on which to base an incentive bonus plan had previously been the firm's office manager. Originally, he had developed systems and accounting reports that had won everyone's compliments because of their actionable form. Based on his sensitivity to the way people use data, he expanded his systems and communication skills as personnel manager of a three hundred and fifty person retail operation.

Almost as a cocktail party game, we have asked managers how they would spend their working lives if, instead of the normal forty years, they had four hundred years to work. Would they do what they are now doing for the whole four hundred years? With practically no exceptions, the answer is that life offers more than being an accountant, running a cement block plant, or supervising forty-five sales representatives selling paper goods. Since you do not have four hundred years, why, if you have the opportunity to change, stay at a job that is unlikely to give you continued satisfaction for forty years?

The change need not be to another company. It can be handled through rotation. In one family company, three fairly equally competent brothers annually rotated the functions of CEO, finance, and marketing. Clearly, no one felt he had to be permanent president. They had a willingness to share decision-making, and a workable arrangement to exchange executive chairs. They were serious about the rotation for two reasons: the quality of key decisions was enhanced because the three executives had broad hands-on knowledge of the total business and they were insuring the company against the loss of any one by providing a responsible backup. The three-person office-of-the-president concept fit their management style.

Third, exchange people with noncompeting firms in the same or related industries. Because it is rarely done, this approach offers an opportunity to develop a special relationship with another firm which might blossom in other ways.

Fourth, a trade or professional association position can be an attractive alternative to boredom. We have known several, usually middle-aged, managers who are able to do the things that require their attention by 10:30 in the morning, but stretch out the available work over the rest of the day. Elected or appointed to responsible jobs in their trade associations, they have applied the energy and intelligence their jobs no longer require to solving association problems. If it offers acclaim and public exposure, requires pleasant or at least tolerable travel, and permits the exercise of power and political skills, the job's benefits can last for a long time.

Two brothers-in-law ran a successful contracting business. The younger, Harry, was the driving force, while John, the older, cleaned up the details Harry often left behind and provided a steady, personal touch. After several years of holding minor association positions, Harry was elected president of the national trade association, a job that traditionally took forty hours a week to perform.

At the end of the year's presidency, the two brothers-in-law reviewed what they and the firm had learned. Harry found that in association work, staffed largely by volunteers, he could not act in the same authoritarian style as he had in his company, rarely restrained by his compliant brother-in-law. He also learned that when he was in his business office his time had to be devoted only to important matters. This required testing of other managers and more delegation, concentration on essentials, and fewer and more pointed reports.

John, the older brother-in-law, also changed his management style. As the on-site owner to whom people turned for answers, he became more decisive and more demanding of people who had previously depended upon his tolerance for mediocrity, and he felt comfortable standing up to Harry. After a day with their five key managers, the two brothers-in-law adjusted their roles and reponsibilities. They resolved that Harry would seek out other activities outside the business to satisfy his need for recognition and power and to accelerate the building of the second management tier.

Harry became active on the local hospital board, the community center, and, after his first taste in politics as treasurer for a friend's successful mayoralty campaign, dropped all other non-business activities to head a group of entrepreneurs who volunteered to apply their skills to improving city government in a Hoover-like commission. Two years later, Harry quit the firm for a full-time political career.

PROMOTION FROM WITHIN

Smaller firms are addicted to promoting from within, and reap the benefits and liabilities of the policy. No firm can afford the consequences of inbreeding, of not refreshing itself by bringing in new ideas and perspectives. A leading source of these perspectives is new employees.

The policy of not hiring from the outside is based on the avoidance of the negative effects of not promoting from within. There are strong reasons to promote from within: ambitious managers can design career paths with reasonable certainty and the company-grown managers know the firm, probably like it, and can act as role models. Because they belong socially and know the people at all levels with whom they have to deal, they will generally be effective in new jobs faster than new people will. But there is an opportunity cost involved: the loss of adding to the firm's inventory of human resources and enriching its pool of talent.

Two comments on the subject follow:

1. If you are going to promote from within, you should have the right raw material. This requires good selection procedures, constant review of potential, testing of people in ways that are not too dangerous to them or the firm, and tough-minded top management willing to admit that early evaluations may have been wrong. In the case of a distributor of industrial supplies, his heir apparent was a close friend who had been in the business for twenty-five years. After members of the firm's advisory committee met the candidate and convinced the owner that his friend would be a disaster, the owner struggled to figure out how to tell his friend and then looked for a replacement. Fortunately, another manager had been growing and, after he was interviewed by a psychologist and the advisory committe, took over the successor's job.

2. When expertise the firm has never had to develop is required, it is usually better to go outside than to grow it internally. However, defining expertise can be tricky. For example, as a retail chain grew, it promoted its best store managers to area supervisors. This promotional policy worked until the company developed over twenty stores in three separate east-coast areas. Local supervisors knew the local regions, but not one of them was adequate to handle the top operating job. The owner wisely brought in a professional from the outside who not only had the executive talent, but also contributed fresh ideas from another background. In areas such as market research, govern-

ment contract negotiations, and the higher levels of computer expertise, finance, and new technology, it is generally faster, cheaper, and safer to buy rather than grow the expertise.

Flexibility in Personnel Strategies

One of the strengths of an effective personnel function is that it is flexible in its policy formulations and applications. It does not have a single set of strategies it applies across the board to personnel. It has different strategies to apply to different people, at different ages, in different economic periods, and so on.

The analogy of product lifecycle may help. Product lifecycle is a basic marketing tool that can be used to indicate the strategies appropriate to a product's position in the cycle. The same strategy does not work at different positions. What works best for a product depends on where it is in its lifecycle. And what has worked best for a product at one position usually damages it when carried over to another position.

Organizational structures and their staffing also go through cycles, although that fact is not widely recognized. And the cycles in smaller firms tend to be shorter than in larger firms, because smaller companies each fill one or not more than several market niches while larger firms often serve more than one major market. Therefore, smaller companies experience greater varieties in size, rate of growth, and personnel needs in shorter periods of time than do larger companies. Consequently, to derive the maximum benefit from their human resources, smaller companies must employ them differently at different times.

Several management consulting firms[3] have demonstrated that different strategies are needed at different points in a firm's growth. Managers in smaller companies are seldom aware of the stage in the organizational lifecycle they are in and, therefore, of how to employ the firm's personnel. We will summarize the different stages and then discuss how selection, performance standards, and compensation should reflect changing company needs.

The Boston Consulting Group identifies different business strategies based on a matrix of market share and market growth. A "business" is any segment of the firm that sells the same products and/or services to a specific market or to different markets.

The Boston Consulting Group matrix has four quadrants, shown

[3]Arthur D. Little, The Boston Consulting Group, and McKinsey & Company.

in Figure 3–1. About 75 percent of all American businesses are in the bottom right, or Dog, category. They have insignificant shares of low or no-growth markets. In the light of inflation and risk, their return on investment of about 15 percent is barely tolerable. They offer few opportunities for growth to ambitious managers who rarely stay after they have gained whatever experience and credentials are available. If the companies are small and closely held, they exist mainly to provide jobs and status to the owners and their families.

The upper right or Question-Mark firm is on the fence. Its managers have a tough decision: although it is in a growing market, the firm has only a small share and is required to invest substantial cash with risky potential returns just to maintain position. The strategic choice is to find a market niche in which the firm can develop a significant share and realize cost reductions through concentrated experience or the profits of a non-commodity marketing position. Without an increase in market share sufficient to move the firm into the Star class, the Question status is hazardous.

The Star is in a desirable position because its high market share and high growth rate combine to produce a high return on investment. Furthermore, since most growth rates eventually slow down, the Star is the usual origin of the fourth category, the Cash Cow. Every company needs a Star as the source of future Stars and to support the Questions which never make it to Star status.

Although there are exceptions to the Boston Consulting Group's classifications, they demonstrate a firm's need to change its personnel practices. Exceptions include the steel industry where the largest steel producer is not the most profitable, specialty auto producers (BMW and Honda are more profitable than Chrysler and British Leyland), and most service industries.

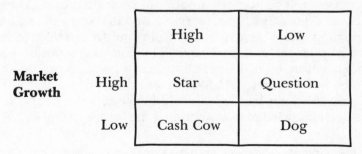

Market Share

	High	Low
Market Growth High	Star	Question
Low	Cash Cow	Dog

Figure 3–1. Matrix of Market Share and Market Growth

The elements of the matrix applicable to personnel policies are growth, ambiguity, risk, measures of success, and compensation. Different stages in the business lifecycle and life of the market require different policies.

Following are examples of personnel policies appropriate to companies or *strategic business units*[4] in each of the four categories.

The manager of a Star would probably have high energy and be extremely ambitious and a leader convinced of his mission's success. He might be imaginative, enthusiastic, quick to exploit market opportunities, competitive, and impatient. The standards by which he should be measured are market share, development of new customers, outlets, and distribution channels. Profits and cash flow might both be negative during the growth stage. Development of a team to support the market is also a proper performance measure. Compensation should be based on medium-to-low base salary and incentives geared to short- and long-range accomplishments.

The short-term measures of his performance should be products developed and shipped, new customers, repeat orders, and hiring of key staff. Long-term objectives might include maintenance or expansion of market share, positive cash flow, acquisition of minor competitors who have started to exploit new niches, and establishment of a management team that would outlast the entrepreneurial manager.

After providing for company needs, the incentive compensation plan should be high, probably limitless. The manager of a Star wants independence, but may need guidance and flexible financial controls to keep him within digestible loss and risk limits. Because he represents the future, his business should be strongly supported.

The Cash Cow requires different people and criteria. The product-service's position has to be supported and expanded. The business's strengths have to be constantly reviewed to reflect changing needs. Basically, the Cash Cow manager is a conservator, willing to change and take risk only within narrow limits. She will enjoy relatively slow growth. Cash flow will be her most important performance measure. Development of adjunct products, services, and markets will require some imagination. Most developments will come from sensitive reactions to new and old customer uses. The company's position as market leader will make it the prime target of competitors, so she will have to be quick to detect flanking moves.

She will probably have had extensive industry experience and can apply bone-deep knowledge to maintaining the business. She will not

[4]*Strategic business unit* is the name given to a division of a larger company serving a single market.

be a major risk-taker. Administratively, she should be dependable because most subordinates will feel comfortable in a secure, largely predictable environment. In order to stay with the changing market, she will have to fight tradition and a desire to leave a good thing untouched.

Her standards of performance should be return on investment, cash flow, maintenance of market position, and successful acquisitions. Her base pay should be above average, and her bonus should not exceed 50 percent of her base. Status and security may be more important than immediate cash returns.

The Question probably requires someone who can handle ambiguity. He should have a strong self-image, since one of his possible options will be to terminate the business. He should be able to handle that probability and long-term frustration. He must stay in touch with the changes the market leader initiates, make fast decisions to respond to emerging opportunities in specialty niches, and be decisive in dropping products, offices, and people as the focus of his division becomes clearer.

His pay should be mid-range with substantial bonuses available. He should not be penalized if the business is terminated. That alternative should be clear from the start of his assignment so that he can consider it without feeling he is committing professional suicide.

His performance measures might be strict adherence to cash commitments and achievement of market share or product acceptance. He should have a lot of flexibility on how he can spend specific amounts with reasonable control over the total. Line-by-line budgeting is inappropriate to the Question or Star.

The Dog manager requires strong support from top management. It is useless to expect competent managers to exert themselves and risk their careers if their business has been damned with the expectation of failure. If they are managed leanly, Dog businesses need not be abandoned. If their marginal income is positive, a holding action can provide training experience for younger managers and a challenge to older ones. A strong, cost-conscious manager is needed.

Even in a non-growth industry, there may be areas of growth and profit to exploit. Fresh analyses of niches and detailed surveys of competitive moves and customer likes might pay off. To keep her cash flow positive, the Dog manager must be willing to try any affordable strategy such as price-cutting or dropping products or services previously considered holy. She should be prepared to sell the business at a price whose present value is greater than the net cash flow to be expected over a reasonable period. Her main talent is the ability to make tough decisions.

Careful monitoring of budgets and tough requirements for any new expenditures put tight restraints on the Dog manager. Pay should be medium to high salary with bonuses based on cash flow, profitable disposition, and the development of younger people.

Basis of the Need

To some, the argument for flexibility in personnel strategy and in the application of human resources as an organization grows smacks of superficiality and sophistry. One fact alone disproves the arguments—the fact that there are no problem-free solutions. Each genuine solution is the substitution of smaller problems for bigger ones. That means the solutions to the problems that arise as companies grow are the causes of the next generation of problems.

Larry Greiner of the Harvard Business School has analyzed how solutions to problems of one organizational stage become the source of problems of the next stage. He found that, as it expands through its early entrepreneurial period, a firm's growth becomes limited by the skills and time of its founder. When those limitations reduce the firm's effectiveness, the owner-manager usually accepts the hiring of a few key people. In a manufacturing company that typically means the addition of production, engineering, marketing or sales, and financial managers. Functional specialization is the first visible sign of professionalism.

Continuing to grow by applying its specialized skills, the firm starts to face problems arising from a lack of coordination and the building of competitive empires. The solution is often a return to centralized decision-making, with its attendant paperwork, controls, and meetings to increase coordination. Having handled the problem of empire-building, the firm now is enmeshed in time-consuming administrative and communication procedures. Managers feel they are constrained and have to fight the bureaucracy. They have lost much of their freedom.

The next step is to decentralize to geographic or product profit centers, develop a headquarters staff, and create detailed budgets and the first long-range plans. Other reactions are extensive use of consultants, management by objectives, detailed organizational charts, and compensation plans based on individual and divisional results. Things look good on paper, the most accepted managerial techniques are applied, but the fun has been pressed out of work. Entrepreneurially inclined managers complain or leave.

The solution is a heavy dose of human resource management. Communication and motivational experts apply their magic. Where possible, a matrix organization is tried. The CEO spends much time listening and making himself visible and available. Individualized pay and benefit plans are installed. Career path counselling and an ombudsman spice up the personnel program. The organization is decentralized as much as economics permit. Each division's marketing and personnel policies are fashioned for individual needs and styles.

Greiner makes a few key points for the smaller company manager who can look forward to struggling through these or similar stages:[5]

1. Like an adolescent, you probably do not know where you are in the growth cycle. Because you have never been through the stage you are in and will be in, you do not know how to handle your current problems.

2. The solution to one stage lays the groundwork for the problems of the next stage.

3. The changes do not come in quantum jumps, but subtly and in ways that at first do not seem to require structural changes, just patching and mending.

4. You will do best to become aware of and handle the changes by getting the advice of outsiders who learn enough about the company to be objective about what is happening.

5. You are not alone. *All* organizations have faced the same growth problems. Although all solutions are not the same, successful companies prepare for change and accept it as natural.

6. Reflect the effects of organizational changes in your management personnel.

Women Managers

In taking an inventory of human resources and determining the adjustments in and additions to the work force needed to meet the goals of the enterprise, smaller firms tend to overlook their female employees.

Approximately forty percent of the working population now is female. Most are employed as non-exempt workers; they do not as yet have proportionate representation in managerial ranks, nor have they yet achieved salary parity with men.

Larger companies have taken the lead in employing women as managers. Smaller companies are lagging in making use of the competence of their female employees or applicants—among other rea-

[5]Larry Greiner, "Evolution and Revolution As Organizations Grow," *Harvard Business Review,* July–August 1972.

sons because of the high tendency to hire males for the less routine, more visible work, and to promote from within (when did you last see a woman hired as a sales representative or appointed production foreman by a smaller company?)

We have encouraged clients to remove the sex barrier to promotions and to include women in their personnel inventories, purely on a cost-effectiveness basis. If, as we believe, an employee represents an investment and is an asset, then the employee should be "worked" at the highest value-adding level possible—regardless of sex. We have never had trouble obtaining acceptance of the principle. But getting the principle implemented is another story.

Keeping subjectivity out of job specifications is difficult. Yet we have seen only one woman of the many we have helped get into higher positions fail, and that was a failure that as easily could have befallen a male—a selection failure. The client (and we) did not do a good job of matching job requirements with the candidate's personality.

When to Recruit

When the human resources inventory has been matched against the latest goals of the firm and the inventory falls short of the skills needed to achieve the results wanted, the firm must go to the outside for personnel.

Although smaller, growing firms cannot avoid recruitment and the people brought into the firm always affect its future performance, smaller companies do not give recruitment high priority—not nearly the importance accorded to it by larger firms. Therefore, they do not get as good people as they would if they had acquired skill in the art of recruiting.

Recruitment is the subject of chapter 5.

4

Appraising Performance

Formal performance evaluation, like testing, has created more fear than pleasure and more negative than positive results in its lifetime. Yet good managers know beyond doubt that knowledge of how an individual is performing is vital to good management. The real problem of performance evaluation is to have its benefits without its harms. Few companies have solved that problem.

The harms are not inherent in the technique. They stem from employing the technique improperly. In this chapter we will share with you our views about how to use performance appraisal to advantage.

Why Performance Should Be Appraised

Performance evaluation may be the most underrated of management tools. Its practical applications are legion. It can be used, for example, in individual development, job design, organization planning, control of turnover, and conflict resolution. When productively conducted, performance evaluation can tidy a field made messy by the natures of people and business. It is the most cost-effective way we know to bring expectations to earth while keeping motivation and cooperation high.

Without reservations, we are in favor of formal appraisal of performance in smaller firms, despite the prevailing view that performance evaluation really belongs in larger firms. We recommend performance evaluation for smaller firms because, having fewer people and less diversity in viewpoint and experience than larger firms, they are more prone to becoming fixed in perceptions of what is important and who does it well than are their larger competitors. Performance appraisals offset that tendency. In one case, a controller's job was saved after an appraisal showed the CEO of an equipment rental company, who conducted the appraisal, that his bias about the controller's initiative and technical skills was groundless.

The quality of a wide range of decisions is improved when they are made on the basis of performance appraisal. For example, the kind of decision whether to promote from within or recruit from the outside benefits from being made on the basis of the appraisal process. Making personnel changes benefits from the input too.

Salaries, for example, should never be changed without honestly and candidly giving the reasons for the changes. How can they be changed with justice to the subjects of the changes *and* other employees without performance appraisals underpinning the changes? People should always know why they are being paid more, or why they are not. To give increases or withhold them *without* giving the reasons for doing so creates fat and happy or disgruntled employees and, ultimately, negates the principle of pay for results. Performance appraisal and compensation adjustments are, therefore, inseparable.

As to frequency, twice a year is useful for new and newly filled positions; once a year for all others is sufficient. As to the timing, we prefer that be established by the dates of employees' last salary adjustments, which means that performance evaluation should precede salary review by a fair amount of time. Some experts say they should be as far apart as possible.

Six months between performance appraisal and salary review may permit discussions about performance, which deals with the future and how the individual can improve, not to be constrained by discussions of the limits of salary levels, which are based on administrative policies and local competitive conditions. Talking about performance in advance of talking about salary gives the supervisor a chance to notify the subordinate about inadequate performance before salary change time. If the subordinate's salary is not changed, the withholding is less shocking.

Evaluations should cover those elements of the job that offer both pay and promotional opportunities. It is usually easier to determine that an employee is ready for promotion than it is to justify a merit increase for doing the same job. Merit rate changes often hang on gray or vague distinctions, whereas readiness for promotion depends on performance differences, which are usually clearer and easier to determine.

Differences in Perceptions of Performance

One of the most difficult problems in appraising performance is dealing with the differences between how people think they are doing and how they are actually doing. People tend to overrate their performances, as several studies have shown. In one study, no one rated himself below the fiftieth percentile. In another, only a small percentage of the employees rated themselves below the seventy-fifth percentile.

Since we know that both talent and performance in most organizations are distributed over a normal curve, the differences between how people think they are doing and how they are actually doing is bound to cause problems. If low performers are not paid in accordance with their perceptions, even when the perceptions are intellectually dishonest, the employees' performance will probably decline further; if they are paid in accordance with their perceptions, the company will be reinforcing unproductive behavior.

The Foundation of Performance Appraisal

The effectiveness of performance appraisals depends more on trust between the boss and the subordinate than on any set of forms and procedures. Add to this tough-minded observation the often-proven fact that people do not benefit from constructive criticism—they resent it. If they hear it at all, they usually defend or excuse their current behavior and find good reasons, in their minds, to continue it.

How, then, can a small company manager improve performance? If trust is the key, then the employee has to believe it is safe and in his best interests to change his performance. The safety factor depends primarily on how consistently he can anticipate his boss's reactions and how much he can depend on the superior's promises to help or support any new behavior.

The relationship is built on specific experience and, therefore, takes time to develop. Until the subordinate has had a chance to develop trust in her boss, it is best to depend on more formal appraisal procedures, which, in effect, can help protect the subordinate from the supervisor's arbitrary or inaccurate evaluations. When trust has been reinforced by daily contact which includes elements of appraisal and evaluation, the formalities are reduced to historical administrative purposes.

Consider the normal MBO list of objectives, usually specific and measurable when properly established. Among professional musicians, these objectives include playing the music as written by the composer or arranger and directed by the conductor. However, music can be played to sound in more than one way even though it is written with unquestioned clarity. Musicians who do not want to work for some group play the music exactly as written and as *they* say they understand the conductor's directions. Since the evaluation of the sounds produced lies entirely in the conductor's head the unhappy musician is told he does not fit and is let go—just as he wanted.

The analogy to a business situation should be clear: the ultimate determination of whether a subordinate is doing a good job, regardless of how specific the performance standards negotiated were, lies in the boss's head. Certainly, the quality of human relationships is largely subjective and the higher we go in the organization, the greater importance we place on those relationships. If the performance appraisal process is to work, the subordinate has to believe that the boss wants him to succeed, will continue to make clear what he wants, will correct deviations in a positive supportive way, and will protect the subordinate from the forces within the company that might prevent him from achieving his goals.

One of the best managers we ever knew said, "My job is to make it easier for my people to do their work." He made this clear in his loyalty, by risking his own neck and providing constant support. The evidence of his trust in his people's ability and their commitment was visible and proved daily.

Improving Performance

Let us reduce a huge amount of literature on how to get people to do better to a few simple rules:

1. Define the job in five to six key, measurable, clear, negotiated results.

2. Provide the resources needed to do the job—people, equipment, money, time, training.

3. Develop fast, accurate feedback, given first to the responsible manager.

4. Make clear in advance what the rewards and punishments will be for success and failure.

5. Provide a consistent, supportive atmosphere.

The first point covers a group of important evaluation and psychological principles—each of the words is significant. No one's job includes more than five or six key results; no one can juggle more than five or six key things simultaneously. Therefore, restrict your performance expectations and your performance reviews to those key items. Note the word *results*—not activities or responsibilities, but results, the things people should be focusing on. *Clear and measurable* results reduce communication differences. *Negotiated* is where commitment comes in. Five pages of clear, measurable objectives initiated by the boss through fiat or fear will not result in the same level of production as an unwritten commitment from the subordinate, which is more likely to come from her emotional involvement in helping set and agreeing to the objectives. Being a participant in setting your own goals results in a stronger commitment than being the passive recipient of someone else's. Results should be listed in priority order to help the employee use her time most effectively.

The second rule requires little comment beyond noting that determining the resources needed to do the job is commonly done superficially. We usually provide the obvious resources of money, equipment, and people, but slight the less obvious ones such as training, time, and introduction to the proper contacts. The lack of these and the other less tangible resources is more commonly the reason for failure than is the lack of tangible resources. Incidentally, authority is not mentioned among the rules because good managers know they never have authority over most of the key factors that affect their fulfilling their responsibility—customers, competitors, the outside world, peers, and their boss. There is rarely a problem concerning the authority a manager has over her subordinates.

Third, the subordinate has to get the information fast and *before* his boss so that he can take corrective action or exploit the opportunity and be prepared to explain what he is going to do or has done. If the subordinate gets the feedback first, the information system becomes part of the supportive structure, since it implies that he is responsible and will take action on his own.

Fourth, we return to the need for rewards (and punishments, which include the denial of rewards) known in advance and considered worthy of the manager's effort and risk of self-esteem. These are able to change performance and therefore are included in a performance appraisal only if they are negotiated.

Finally, people are willing to do more, show initiative, occasionally strike out, and challenge the firm's holies, including the boss's prejudices, in an environment in which they feel confident of the boss's reactions to their actions. A consistent, supportive atmosphere improves the possibility that the employee will perform as you want.

Appraisal Conflicts

There are some conflicts inherent in the appraisal system. The firm wants to: (1) improve employees' performance and assumes that feedback on how the person is doing will be used to correct behavior; and (2) develop objective information to make pay and promotion decisions.

These goals are evaluative and put the supervisor in a judgmental role. At the same time, the firm wants to counsel the employee, strengthen commitment to the firm by laying out possible career paths, improve one-on-one relations, and identify problems.

The conflict lies in the difficulty of the employee's maintaining a strong self-image while the organization presents negative information with the expectation that doing so will result in improved performance. Since it is extremely difficult to criticize constructively, both parties to an appraisal session approach the process with trepidation. The employee does not feel comfortable being totally open because he knows that in her evaluative, judgmental role the supervisor may use the information against him in salary and promotion decisions.

The supervisor may feel uncomfortable because she is unable to separate her two roles. Since the bulk of her daily relationship with her subordinate is as a coach and counselor, she is aware, consciously or intuitively, that, when she puts on her judgmental hat, she is likely to affect the personal relationship she has taken great care to develop. The result is a mutual holding-back, neither party feeling free to be open, and a conversation that is either perfunctory or rambles around the point.

Appraisal Solutions

Some possible solutions are:

1. Separate the evaluation and coaching sessions by making it clear that they are different and will be handled differently.
2. Choose performance measures that are objective and agreed

upon in advance. Avoid all generalizations. If a negative performance is brought up, it should be specific. It is damaging and, even more important, useless to tell someone he lacks initiative. Better to say, "When customer A said he was unhappy with our product, instead of sympathizing, apologizing, and leaving it at that, you might have found out what specifically we could do to make him happy. Then you could have brought the information back to those in the company who could use it." Instead of saying that someone is insensitive to people, say "When Mary came in late three days in a row, instead of yelling at her, you might have asked her what her problem was. As you learned, her son was seriously ill and she had to pick up a baby-sitter so that she could come to work at all."

3. Handle each person as an individual. This means that each should have a separate method of being appraised. The forms can be the same, but the timing, the amount of self-appraisal, and who does most of the talking will vary. Some people want appraisal mainly as a confirmation from the organization of what they know about themselves and to get information on where they are going. Others need constant reinforcement.

4. Appraisals done from two unusual directions may help: an upward appraisal by the subordinate of her boss and a self-appraisal that precedes the dialogue. The upward appraisal introduces an element of democracy into a usually one-way relationship. The self-appraisal usually results in a lower evaluation than the supervisor would provide, because the employee does not want to present her boss with an evaluation which will be seen as self-serving, thereby negatively affecting the boss's perception. With experience and proper use, self-appraisal can be an objective way to start the discussion.

5. Self-appraisals and upward appraisals are examples of getting employees involved in the evaluation process. Both are after the fact. More important is regular subordinate involvement in goal-setting and problem-solving, perhaps using management by objectives.

6. Place the appraisal interviews in the context of the supervisor-subordinate relationship. If daily contact has been healthy and aimed primarily at improving the employee's performance, the annual or semi-annual formality is just one milestone in the process. Not only are "constructive" and "criticism" incompatible, more criticism usually results in lower performance. The employee sets lower goals to avoid further damage to his self-

image. A more effective approach is problem-solving, based on a supportive atmosphere and an attempt to deal with the problems mutually.

7. Do not use peer comparisons to make important judgments. If the number of individuals in the group being compared is small, it is unlikely you will have a normal distribution of talent and performance. Such comparisons may be helpful in making promotion decisions, but they are useless in appraisals. What can a person do about improving his performance if he is told that he is fifth out of eight in his peer group? The damaging effects of this type of appraisal are that an internally destructive competition may be set up and the individuals have no idea of where they stand in terms of their own quality of work.

Although some rewards are limited and of zero-sum nature (only one vice-president of sales, only so many dollars available for raises or bonuses), others are not. Recognition, challenge, satisfaction from the work itself, time off, and other rewards can be individually designed. If financial rewards are a key part of the results of the appraisal system, search for ways that everyone can make more but not at each other's expense. The best plans do not pit employees against each other, but against competitors. If the firm earns more, everyone benefits.

Appraising the Appraisal

BFS Psychological Associates, Inc., New York, N.Y., in its periodical *Interaction,* has prepared a short test of the appraisal system, which they suggest be conducted by a trained interviewer, preferably a psychologist, after employees have gone through the appraisal. Here are the questions:

1. How often have you been appraised during the last three years?
2. What was discussed? Specifically, what did you learn about:
   a. how your supervisor feels about your current performance, your future growth?
   b. what you can or should do for future growth and development?
   c. short and long term goals of the company and your job?
3. Are you satisfied with what you learned from the above questions?

4. Were you free to express your opinions? How would you like to express your opinions in the future?
5. How did your supervisor show concern in making the appraisal:
   a. How long did it last?
   b. Did the supervisor take the appraisal seriously or just go through the motions?
6. Do you agree with the results of the appraisal? If not, why not? Did you feel comfortable differing openly with the appraiser?
7. Are you planning to make any changes in what you do as a result of the appraisal? What changes? Did you make any changes as a result of the last appraisal? (If the answers to these questions are negative, you should seriously question whether the performance goals of the process are being achieved.)
8. What were the biggest problems in your last appraisal?
   a. lack of adequate data
   b. lack of personal input; no chance to talk, just listen
   c. tension surrounding the appraisal
   d. other
   How would you correct these problems?

Performance measurement and appraisal are part of the trio of things every employee wants to know:

1. What is my job—what am I supposed to do? This question is answered in a position description and list of key results expected.
2. How well am I supposed to do it? This question is answered by negotiated standards of performance.
3. How am I doing? This is where the performance appraisal fits in.

By clearly understanding and agreeing to the first two elements, the employee is protected from arbitrary and mysterious evaluations. The boss's purely subjective appraisal is replaced by objective standards. Traits and ambiguous criteria are replaced by job effectiveness in as measurable terms as possible. An example of a performance appraisal form which ties together these elements is shown in Figure 4–1.

The form in Figure 4–1, or one modified for your own use, is simple, clear, objective, and, if backed with specific evidence of performance, can be the effective focus for an appraisal session. It is

Name   **Position**

Supervisor's name   **Date**

Critical responsibility areas (in priority order)

Targeted objectives (for each area)

Results realized (for each area)

Rating for each critical responsibility area (outstanding, satisfactory, unsatisfactory)

Signatures:

Employee _____

Supervisor _____

Figure 4–1. Sample Performance Appraisal Form

also appropriate for a self-appraisal, which would precede a supervisor-subordinate dialogue.

Merit Raises

Although many organizations have an announced policy of distributing pay increases on merit, employees often see the increases as given independent of performance, based on seniority, the cost of living, or a formula blind to differences in individual contribution. That is unfortunate. When everyone receives a 5 percent raise, the ones you hurt the most are those who have contributed the most. If you want to keep your top producers around and keep them producing, fashion individual pay programs for them.

Merit pay's limitations are its tendency toward bias, inadequate information on the part of the supervisor who disburses the rewards, and evaluations that substantiate rather than determine salary changes. Merit raises are not for key people.

Since payroll dollars available for merit pay or performance bonuses are limited, most employees will be consistently disappointed by their pay increases. In most cases, objective analyses of performance show a few key people performing extremely well, most doing an adequate, expected job, and a few performing marginally.

Another problem with merit appraisals is that they are rarely oriented toward job results. More often, the ratings are based on such traits as friendliness, helpfulness, loyalty, and intelligence, which are not only hard to define but are often totally irrelevant to the performance.

In summary, a merit system will probably keep most people happy. However, it will not help you retain outstanding performers and will not do much to motivate and change the behavior of people by relating rewards and performance.

5 ❧
Recruiting

Bringing people in from the outside is not one of the things smaller firms generally do well. They tend to perform the work under the handicaps of inexperience, a sense of inferiority to larger companies, and unrealistic perceptions of job qualifications. This chapter offers some views on how smaller firms can get more for their recruiting efforts.

Recruit from Strength

Smaller company managers often feel they are at the low end of the list of places competent people want to work. They tend to be apologetic in offering jobs to applicants who are obviously qualified to work in larger companies.

It is true the smaller companies are unattractive to job applicants still gripped by the aged notion that security and opportunity are largely derived from working in larger organizations. But these people are a shrinking group. Many well-qualified people today want to work in the smaller company because of its appreciable size-related advantages. How well the smaller company interviewer seeks out the personal aspirations and needs of the candidate and matches them with those advantages is often the deciding factor in the individual's final choice of employers.

Therefore, in recruitment, start out with the feeling that good people can be attracted to the smaller company. True, good people have the widest choice of places to work. Even when the general economic situation is tough and jobs are scarce, the best people usually have a choice. They are the ones employers compete for. But that does not say that good people prefer big companies. Our recent experiences show the opposite. In our recruitment work we have found good people to be opportunity rather than size oriented and to be attracted more to the degree of autonomy they will be afforded, the flexibility of the reward system, and the possibility of capital accumulation than to employment and career security.

There are good reasons for getting the best people. Good people are not expensive, although you will usually have to pay them at the high part of the salary range for the job. They find quicker and better solutions to problems, make fewer mistakes, and require less training and supervision than less competent people. They probably work harder, but they almost certainly will work smarter. They may cost more on a dollar-per-hour basis, but will cost less when measured against output, return on investment, or unit of result.

Hiring less than the best will shortly prove the old proverb: Mediocrity breeds mediocrity. Few things will frustrate a competent employee more quickly and thoroughly than having to work daily with a mediocre co-worker. If you have five highly competent people and five mediocre ones in peer positions, the competent ones, not the mediocre ones, will quit in frustration or boredom. Soon, the mediocre people will dominate the organization.

Do not stint on recruitment. Money spent intelligently at the front end of selection cannot possibly approach the costs of defective recruitment.

In a large public accounting organization, about 1,500 young graduates were hired annually. Over one-half left by the end of the second year. The estimated cost of that loss was $7.5 million. One of the authors interviewed several of the ex-employees to find out why they had left. The main reason was disillusionment. The glamor, status, professional growth, and intrinsic satisfaction that had been promised or implied during the recruitment interviews had not been realized. For example, in one case, a crew of young auditors had worked seven days a week, twelve hours a day, in the vault of a bank, counting securities. To save time, lunch was brought in, and the only way to leave the vault during working hours was to go to the bathroom. It was impossible to reconcile weeks of this low-level, excruciatingly boring (if necessary) work with the image of a professional accountant resolving high-level problems with the financial vice-president of a publicly held company, offering money-saving advice to an entrepreneur, or giving evidence in a spectacular court case.

Set Correct Hiring Standards

While smaller companies do not have to take a back seat in hiring good people, it is plain that larger companies do have certain advantages. But smaller firms have advantages over larger ones in several respects; they can be more flexible as to age, education, and opening offers.

Unlike large companies, small firms should be little concerned with a candidate's credentials, the schools she attended, the companies she worked for, her titles, or the style of her presentation. Smaller firms should be primarily concerned with the *quality* of a candidate's prior *experience*. Nothing is better as a predictor of how successfully she will perform. Prior performance in a comparable job is more a factor in job success in smaller companies than in larger ones, where the ability to get along with people is as important as the way a job is done.

Smaller companies may be better looking for people who are old enough to have had the broader experience normally required. Larger companies can use younger, narrow specialists who are not experienced outside their immediate job responsibilities. We recommend that smaller companies look to hire older people who, because of their wider knowledge, can produce and be tested sooner and are more likely to start their jobs with confidence.

We had an experience that confirmed this observation. A manufacturer of specialty metal and plastic products was looking for a manufacturing-engineering vice-president. In checking the references of one of the attractive candidates who was in his mid-fifties, we learned that he had been asked to leave a recent job because his previous employer had decided his company needed a person knowledgeable about computers. The candidate was not interested in spending the time becoming expert in computers and was, therefore, looking for another job. For the smaller company, the computer deficiency was not a factor in filling the job, while the candidate's thirty-five years of manufacturing experience could be put to immediate use.

Defining the Market

In recruitment, smaller companies need to be sensitive to the conditions within their employment markets. We use the plural because they are affected both by the local geographical market and the broadest job market as defined by current and potential employees.

For example, if you are hiring unskilled workers in a metropolitan area, your competition is every other unskilled job opening in that area, not just the competitor in your industry. A cement block plant in the south, the only one within a seventy-five-mile radius, could not retain workers to handle their block machines. Why would a worker do a dull job in a block plant at four dollars an hour when he could get a dull job in a paper mill at five dollars an hour?

A computer software firm in Minneapolis thought it was competing for programmers and system analysts with every firm offering a comparable job in the northern mid-west. But, since technical workers have almost complete job mobility, it was really competing for personnel on a national basis. It is unlikely that the company would be interesting to competent workers in the local area who had decided to live in the Boston, Southern California, or New York areas.

Comparability extends along job lines, particularly where the job is seen as professional. The definition of a professional has been widened in recent years. Where formerly a professional was defined as a lawyer, engineer, accountant, or doctor, today professionals include managers of marketing, finance, warehousing and distribution, human resources and personnel, and the whole field of data processing. Providing time for people to acquire the specialized knowledge, designing reinforcing career experience paths, and expecting less than a lifetime of work in a single company are characteristics of a profession. The main reason for this change in employer-employee attitude is that the professional feels he owes his loyalty to his profession more than to his employer.

Selection of Managers

A key profit-improving idea we want to emphasize is the relative importance of selection over training, compensation, human relations programs, organizational design, or almost any other managerial decision-making area except market focus. Simply stated, the person you hire is the person with whom you are going to work. If they have the abilities and the interest, you can teach people where the debits and credits are, the difference between a crane and a bulldozer, how to fill out an insurance form, how to weld metal, saw wood, cut cloth, repair telephones, and other necessary skills. But because managerial skills are harder to define and teach, because we rarely ask why people fail in managerial jobs, and because many managers think they know how to pick a good person, the highest failure rate, largest turnover, and biggest waste and risk is in hiring or promoting managers. The welder rarely fails because he does not know how to weld, the carpenter is not fired because he cannot put nails in the board, the secretary because he cannot type. Simple tests of the skill levels required are available. Because they are valid and reliable (they test what we expect them to and they do so consistently), it is foolish not to use them in hiring when success is largely related to skill or knowledge.

Managers, however, usually fail for other, usually non-technical, reasons. A leading source of the failures is conflict between the needs of the job and of the inborn personality traits of the person in the job. Few people are natively endowed to deal with stress, ambiguity, interpersonal relations, or to recognize the difference between problem-solving and problem-finding. A few examples may help explain why people who seem to have all the necessary experience and skills sometimes do not work out.

A project manager who had been successful in handling the largest jobs of a construction company was promoted to supervisor of project engineers, a job that required him to monitor and support ten project engineers, who between them handled up to fifty jobs at a time. The supervisor was unable to balance the number of people, the different time pressures, and the variety of jobs.

A vice-president of operations who had always been in control of purchasing, production, quality control, and shipping and receiving began to be short-tempered, take long lunches, and be absent for illness. What had brought about this behavior? The company's move to a long-range planning mode had added responsibilities to his job. A person able to cope with any problem as long as it was here and now could not cope with what to him was abstract.

A bookkeeper who was doing a good job of ledger-keeping and was regarded as a pleasant, even-tempered worker was promoted to manage credit and collection. Soon after, customers began to complain to company sales representatives or stop buying. In her new job, the formerly quiet bookkeeper had turned tough, belligerent, and inflexible.

STRESS

Stress can be described as a psychological dysfunction rising out of the recognition or fear that one cannot cope. It is in the individual, not in the job. Nevertheless, jobs cause stress when they are not well matched to the incumbent's abilities. Having to deal with many factors, jobs, or people under deadlines is a principal source of stress. Some people are superb at handling a single job—they can concentrate, and get the single job done on time and within specifications, but cannot handle a situation with many variables. Stress is not limited to selected work: professionals, managers of diverse numbers of projects or people, housewives, all have the same exposure to setting priorities and being able to juggle and balance. Since few job descriptions mention the stress aspect of a position, it is usually mysterious when the person successful in one type of job fails in the stressful one. The opposite situation may cause poor performance: some people, bored only by repetitive activity, *need* challenge, and variety. Quickwitted, energetic people are wrong for jobs that take patience and concentration. Be sure of a match between job and psychological characteristics in your recruitment specifications.

AMBIGUITY

Ambiguity seems to be directly proportionate to the level in the organization: the higher up you go, the more it increases. Certainly, the further up in the organization, the harder it is to find specific measures for evaluating how you are doing in the total job. For example, CEOs of small companies can easily measure their return on investment, and actual results versus budget in sales and costs and comparisons with industry statistics. However, as every top manager who has thought about her job knows, there are elements of her job on which the long-range survival of her company depends that are not precise—such as loyalty of customers, commitment of key people, product life cycle, effect of social and economic trends, and the relationship between her own goals and the needs of the firm. Where you stand and how you are doing in relation to these key factors are almost always ambiguous evaluations. The sales representative sells or does not; the engineer finishes the drawing for the new product or process and it works or it does not. But the supervisor of the sales representative and of the engineer has to deal with the quality of his relationship with his subordinates and the level of imagination and creativity he can expect. Long-range planning becomes complicated in inverse proportion to company size. In other words, the smaller the company, short of firms too small to need any long-range planning, the more uncertainties enter the process of anticipating and trying to survey and benefit from future events. We think it best that smaller firms go slowly in formalizing the details of plans beyond a few years. Yet smaller companies need a sense of direction as much as larger ones do. Picking a course in a changing, competitive environment means dealing with a great number of uncertainties, a state of mind which leaves many people uncomfortable.

HANDLING PROBLEMS

Managers are more often complimented for solving problems than for any other accomplishment. Note the number of resumes in which the applicant boasts of his problem-solving ability. There is even the managerial parody of the manager who announces to his spouse as she hands him the arrival-at-home cocktail that he solved forty-six problems today, four more than yesterday. The truth is that, although solving problems is necessary to stay on course and to prevent the firm from falling apart, it is not the highest level of management skill. Having solved a problem, where are you? At best, where you were before the problem, minus the time, effort, and diversion of managerial skill required to bring things back to where they were supposed to be in the first place.

Rarer and more important is skill in *finding* problems, discovering the problems that are hidden from view or are misrepresented and that are therefore misinterpreted in analysis. Since managers are most often brought into the limelight by their ability to solve problems, get the work out, and handle people, it is usually assumed that the best problem-solvers will make the best top managers. Not so—the best problem solvers probably belong where they are right now, solving problems in operations at all levels. They are often poor, sometimes disastrous, candidates for top management positions in which they must deal with tomorrows rather than with todays.

Top managers are supposed to be looking to the future. In small firms, they need administrative skills to plan and get out the work, but they are most valuable when they have the ability to step away from the satisfaction of a problem solved and move into the intellectually more demanding realm of the future. The gap between the skills of problem solving and finding often explains why successors do not do as well as founders. Founders succeed because they made the original decisions, which were good for the time but also the seeds of many problems to come. Successors are usually chosen because they have made their mark by straightening things out. Every firm needs both talents, but at the top it needs *original* decision-making far more than *corrective* decision-making. We want to emphasize that when you define the job of a top manager you include in the specifications the level of initiative required.

It is not easy to test for problem-finding skill, since, like adolescence, it is hard to describe until you have been through it. Asking questions and looking for examples of the experiences a person feels represent him at his best may reveal a self-image and history (able to be checked) and identify capacity beyond problem-solving. Willingness to take risks, imagination, creativity, challenging the routine, and persistence in following through are characteristics that reveal the problem-finder.

INITIATIVE

Related to the problem-handling characteristics is the level of following routine or showing initiative. Although top managers often say they want tigers around them—that is, challengers, questioners, and idea people—they would probably be extremely uncomfortable in the daily presence of too many tigers. Just as armies need to have dependable soldiers who follow rational orders to run successfully, so companies need a working level of consensus and agreement to do what is needed to satisfy the customer after the basic mission has been set.

Equally, any business organization that asks for slavish obedience is doomed. Practical ideas and improvements should be encouraged from everyone and considered openly. However, when all ideas have been filtered and a final decision has been made, the job has to be done as decided. At lower levels, many jobs are plain dull. Hiring over-competent people for dull jobs is bad for everyone. As Saul Gellerman has said, hire dull people for dull jobs and provide social and other amenities for them so they can derive satisfaction from employment aside from the work itself.

Some jobs are best done as laid out. Other jobs, especially those dealing with customers and change areas, are done best when initiative is allowed and encouraged. The outstanding management contribution of a McDonald's has been to rationalize service by limiting the number of choices available to their several hundred thousand, largely part-time, young workers. McDonald's behavior does not contradict the point; the firm has routinized the service function so that product delivery and quality are uniform throughout the system. The company cannot formalize the personal contact between the employee and the customer nor, except to the extent of standard wording, greetings, and requests for additional items, does it try.

Since people differ in the levels of routine they can tolerate and initiative they need to exercise, again, to improve selection results, define the levels of each involved in the job, and interview and test to match the levels with the developed personalities.

INTERPERSONAL COMPETENCE

The last among the sources of job failure we have described as typical and to which we caution you be sensitive is interpersonal competence. Compare the interpersonal skills required of sales representatives with those of their manager. In most selling situations today, where decisions are increasingly being made to obtain economic advantage rather than personal gratification, a sales representative's personality must at least not be alienating. That is, he should be able to deal with customers and prospects so he does not alienate them. It is unlikely that industrial and much retail and personal service selling is completed on the basis of charm and good looks. We do not downgrade the effect of these fortuitous strengths, but think they have little influence at the point of sale. The sales representative's interpersonal competence should be good enough to enable her to make her presentation without hindrance, bring out and solve customer problems, get the customer to reveal his real and imagined concerns, and create acceptance of her product or service. Certainly, this short and incomplete list of a sales representative's skills shows the importance of interpersonal skill. But as interpersonal talents they are superficial compared to those required of a manager who has long, continued, productive, and unavoidable contact with a small group of subordinates.

The sales representative can choose not to deal with a customer with whom he does not get along or who he finds objectionable, in many cases, by getting the customer transferred (especially where personal chemistry is the problem). If he is independent and has some choice of customer calls, he can drop the customer entirely because he has decided that work has to offer a balance between what you give and get. The manager does not have those options, at least not to the same degree.

Perhaps these comments will explain why so few sales representatives become good sales managers, why so few expert accountants become good administrators of large accounting departments, and why most great baseball and football managers and tennis coaches were not great players. The skills in each job are different. Therefore, when you define a managerial job, do not make the mistake of defining it in terms of the skills required of the group below. Define the interpersonal skills required at the managerial level and expand your recruitment beyond those who have done the work itself well. Do not eliminate the best producer or most expert person. Just do not make the dangerous mistake of assuming that the skills at one level are the best qualifications for a job at the next. That raises the issue of how to reward the good worker who focuses on doing the work well and thereby may deprive himself of the chance to develop the qualifying skills of the good manager or of the next higher job level. We will comment on this dilemma later in the book.

All of these cautions about job definition and selection may make the successful filling of a managerial position sound impossible. Not so—heeding the cautions assures at the least greater success in filling most positions. Considering the costs of filling jobs, even a small improvement pays off. The exception are jobs that are so difficult their definition is useless. These undoable jobs exist where a boss will not tolerate a strong subordinate or successor, or where the job has grown by accretion, usually because the person holding it is competent and naturally attracts every loose responsibility floating by. Eventually, the competence is overtaxed by the volume of responsibilities acquired and by the fact that some of them are inherently contradictory.

In one company, a design engineer position was to be filled. Among the specifications were customer research, competitor analysis, design and tooling of new products, process engineering, quality control, training sales representatives, writing technical journals, and customer service. Only when the president reviewed the list (the first time he had seen it) did he see that the job was undoable. The reason four apparently good people had failed in the last few years was not attributable to their inadequacy or to selection. The job demanded a wider range of skills and experiences than were likely ever to be found in one person. Where possible, ask the person leaving a job to list all the results for which she is responsible—not the things she does, only the *results*. The list will be helpful in defining the type of person you will need to fill the job next time.

Employment Testing

We have always been advocates of employment testing, psychological testing, or testing by any other name that is employed in an honest effort to connect job requirements with skills.[1] Employment testing is under attack, however. The publicity created by legal difficulties and attacks on the grounds of discrimination has cost employment testing some of its hard-won acceptance. But behavioral scientists have not found any alternatives to testing. When tests are used under conditions of proven validity, care for legal limitations, and appropriateness of application, they can improve selection and productivity.

[1]We use tests both in our recruiting work and in conducting personnel inventories. The latter, of course, consists in assessing employees for increased contribution and developmental needs.

Most large companies test. But companies with fewer than one hundred employees use tests little more than one-third of the time, largely at the lowest hiring levels. The trend has been away from testing. Government rules and exposure to possible suits have caused many companies to drop testing rather than to try to understand and observe the rules. We favor the latter course of action.

For example, a firm manufacturing a complex surgical device became subject to governmental regulation. The owner's first reaction was to avoid the problem by selling the business. Later, he was convinced that, although adhering to the regulations might be a chore, it was wiser to deal with them than to sacrifice the business. The solution was to hire a legally trained assistant who took the burden off the owner so that he was able to devote his time to building the business, which he was able to do very successfully.

Testing offers the same opportunities. Learn the rules, what can be done, what tests are acceptable, and then use tests that separate ability levels to reduce your selection mistakes.

A major misunderstanding in the use of tests is that tests discriminate against groups on the basis of race or national origin. Not so— tests do not discriminate any more than computers steal. In both cases, it is people who do the dirty work. How the test is used, not the nature of the test or results, is the source of any bias or prejudice. Hiring includes a great number of inputs. Be concerned with the whole process of hiring so that it will be fair. Testing fits into the process, but should not be treated as a separate, unrelated item.

If a test used in a single company shows differences between people of different races, it would be unscientific to conclude that there are such differences in the general population. Rarely does a single company have a sufficient number of randomly chosen test results to justify a scientific conclusion. Furthermore, it is critical to the test's validity and any employment conclusions made from the results to analyze other factors that could cause the results.

For example, a survey showed that, on a per capita basis, Jews had the highest income in the country and Puerto Ricans the lowest. When it separated the age factor, the survey showed that the Jews had the highest proportion of older people, that Puerto Ricans had the highest proportion of young people, and that there was a direct relationship—independent of religion, race, and almost everything else— between age and income. Older people make more money than younger. Employment tests may test traits or skills which are unrelated to a racial or religious background but which may be related to education, opportunity, or economic background.

Because tests imply accuracy they are an easy target for attacks on their validity. Validity means that a test measures what it is supposed to. Supporters of tests properly ask: "What methods are used to validate the alternatives to tests?" Typical alternatives are interviewing and reviews of resumes. Interviews are notoriously poor in improving selection. If anything, they are probably more subject to bias than testing, since it is impossible to validate the results of an interview by any statistically adequate means.

Experience and education information in resumes is assumed to be relevant to successful hiring. Although common sense might suggest that prior experience and education are pertinent to job success, there is little real evidence in job experience. Furthermore, by putting educational and experience limitations on job applications, a company excludes those who have been denied job and educational opportunities, usually for economic reasons.

Assessment centers, used for the most part by large companies, have shown some success in predicting job performance, but are expensive and largely useful in filling managerial positions.

We return to testing as one of the more dependable sources of information about applicants. Validity is the first criterion: does the instrument test what it is supposed to? Does it separate the high, average, and low performers? Is there a direct, provable relationship between test results and performance on the job? If the answers are positive, you have a useful device.

SELECTING A TEST

Price and ease in administration are important considerations in choosing tests. Self-marking tests are particularly attractive. Those administered frequently enough to allow a company to build up its own history are also useful. Tests must also observe the rules and not be subject to attack by minority groups claiming discrimination, even when none is intended.

It should be clear that the choice, administration, and interpretation of tests are jobs for professionals. Find a local psychologist or testing service who can get to know your company and the jobs you are trying to fill. Have some of your best, average, and below-average employees take the test to see whether it separates performance in *your* organization, and then add testing to your arsenal of selection tools.

In addition to the tests listed below, the psychologists we have worked with use specific tests for special groups: sales representatives, personnel managers, engineers, and technical writers. The responsible test analyst reviews all available information about the company and, if possible, visits with the key personnel and interviews the candidates. Tests should be interpreted by qualified professionals, preferably licensed psychologists who specialize in the testing field. Examples of useful tests are: the Ship Destination, Logical Reasoning, and Concept Mastery tests and the Edwards Personal Preference Schedule.

Ship Destination Test. This test measures intelligence as manifested in concrete, but increasingly complex, situations involving primarily the ability to reason within a numeric, readily quantifiable situation.

Logical Reasoning Test. This is a difficult test that measures abstract, logical reasoning at the highest level and under stressed (timed) conditions. The subject has to separate the process of abstract, syllogistic, and logical reasoning from content, personal bias, and interpretation through the information itself. Usually, people tend to blend the two elements and arrive at decisions they think are based exclusively on logical appraisal but are, in fact, highly dependent upon feelings, hunches, and knowledge about the subject. This may be perfectly appropriate, but it is obviously helpful to be able to separate out the two components.

Concept Mastery Test. This is a test of applied intelligence which stresses ability to reason abstractly and develop logical relationships, but in a setting that is very much dependent upon education covering a broad spectrum of areas: vocabulary, cultural knowledge, general education, scientific information, literary ability, and so forth. This test is particularly appropriate for top management.

Edwards Personal Preference Schedule. This test provides a convenient measure of fifteen relatively independent personality variables found in normal individuals. These cover such factors as the need to achieve, the importance placed upon exhibition of one's assets, the need for support, the ability to endure, the tendency to change, and an individual's basic aggressiveness.[2]

We had an experience with subjective feelings about quality levels in hiring a manufacturing vice-president. The company made a single product that was used world-wide. The rejects from first-quality standards were sold in countries where the company's rejects were better than anything locally available. It made economic sense to divide the production into two quality categories and sell the second in desig-

[2]The section on available tests is based on information supplied by Cyril M. Franks, Ph.D., Distinguished University Professor at the Graduate School of Applied and Professional Psychology, Rutgers University, New Brunswick, N.J.

nated markets. Because the product unacceptable in the U.S. was sought in other areas, the company saw no reason to sell the two products at different prices. What we found difficult to get across to the CEO who had lived with this situation for thirty years was that he might have trouble hiring a manufacturing vice-president to whom the sale of second-grade product at the same price as first-grade was not an economic or marketing issue, but a moral or ethical one. The selection process for success on that job required someone with the flexibility to understand the company's position.

Define the job in traditional terms of the types of functions required in handling information, people, and things. Managerial candidates are heavy on information and people skills and light on things. The more precise you can be in describing each of the functions the better the fit you will get. Typical words used in information handling might be comparing, computing, analyzing, and creating. People skills might include hiring, teaching, monitoring, persuading, firing, and cooperating with. Each job will probably have a different priority for each function. List them in priority, giving specific examples, if you can, of exactly what a good performance would mean. Here are examples for a sales manager in an equipment distribution business.

Using the results approach:

Sell _____ units at _____ percent gross margin for each major product line

Open _____ new accounts and sell them at _____ gross margin dollars

Hire _____ new sales representatives and have them productive at the end of the year so that their earnings equal their draw and expenses

Maintain sales costs within 5 percent of the variable budget

Prepare a sales plan for the coming year by December 1

Using the data, people, things approach:

Data: Prepare sales projections for each major product line; show gross margin in dollars and percentages and sales targets by customers

Prepare sales projections by markets, areas, end-users; show potential of each with probability of success

Report monthly on action taken with variances—plus or minus— in excess of 10 percent of projection or budget

Prepare analysis of our product lines versus competitors'

People: Hire _____ sales representatives (same as above under Results)

Handle all sales representatives' training and personnel matters

Develop staffing projection for next three years showing potential of each sales representative and steps to be taken to strengthen performance through training or on-the-job experience

Things: Be familiar enough with major equipment to be able to demonstrate it in the field to potential customers

Although the second approach is more detailed, another dozen specific tasks could be added to the job description. We prefer the results approach because it is limited by the nature of *all* jobs. We have never been able to come up with more than six significant result areas to measure *any* job, from the head of a country to a vice-presidency or foreman in a small company. Describing a job in results for selection purposes not only focuses interviewing, reference-checking, and other information-seeking, it provides a natural transition from the selection and hiring steps to the job itself. People cannot balance, juggle, or set priorities on more than five or six things. Combine this psychological observation with the limits on the number of job results and you have a good reason for tying in the half-dozen measures used to define a job with the model concept.

We proposed that all successful companies have some market uniqueness. Having identified that uniqueness with sufficient specifics so that it is clear and actionable, you have the structure around which to build a job description in key result areas. As an example, consider the mechanical contractor to whom the word "claim" by a customer was unknown. His business was built on the premise that the customer had to be satisfied. The job had to be done within time, quality, and cost specifications that would leave the customer happy enough to recommend the contractor to others and make it almost instinctive to turn to him for the next job. The economics of this approach were simple: the contractor avoided the pitched battles typical of the industry in which a low bid was the only way to get business. All of his contracts were negotiated, typically at prices 3 to 5 percent above competitive figures. Sophisticated customers were willing to pay the premium because the contractor's insistence on timely, accurate work eliminated a layer of follow-up and supervision on the part of the owner or general contractor. Traditionally, 80 percent of his work in any year came from owners or general contractors with whom he had worked previously.

With this background and clear market strategy, it was fairly easy to define the results required at every managerial and technical level; it was also simpler to hire people when certain personality leanings and needs could be identified as especially fitting or unlikely to succeed. For example, candidates with a background of competitiveness, who were eager to boast how they had taken advantage of customers or general contractors, whose basic approach to life was combative, or who saw business situations as win-lose choices, were clearly unfit to deal with customers or to supervise field workers.

When to Use Personnel Recruiters

Size affects the decision to use personnel recruiters, just as it does most personnel decisions.[3] Smaller firms should use personnel recruiters more often than they do. Even with their professional personnel staffs, large companies turn to recruiters to fill many technical and managerial jobs. It may be even more important for small companies to use a recruiter's services, because the few key people in a small company are individually more important than they are in a large firm. Recruiters are responsible for directing the right people to a company. Although the cost of the recruiter may seem substantial to a small firm, it may be inconsequential compared to the impact of the right key person—technician, first-line manager, or top officer on the company's long-range future.

Smaller companies should be sure the personnel recruiter understands its management and working style, since a personality fit is more important in small than large companies. One rarely mentioned difficulty in the switch from a large to a small firm is the absence in the latter of the staff help on which a large firm manager routinely calls. In the small firm, the manager has to be ready to do the whole job himself, or scrounge for help.

Because the cost of hiring is so great, small firms should look for reasonable tenure in their hiring and make that intent clear to the personnel recruiter.

When should smaller companies use a recruiter? They are probably most valuable recruiting people from the two to three year professional level and up. There are three distinct components of the personnel service business, each with a different expertise. Choose the one who is most likely to help solve your specific job need. The employment agent functions primarily in the first-line administrative, secretarial, and entry-level professional area. The contingency re-

[3]This section is based on material supplied by Rolfe Kopelan, President, Human Resource Management, Inc., New York, N.Y.

cruiter concentrates on the three-year and up professional and technical level, and middle and upper-middle management. The executive search consultant works on jobs at the vice-presidential, divisional manager level and up.

To find a recruiter, look in a newspaper or trade magazine for firms that advertise in the specialty, professional, or managerial areas in which you are interested. Call a larger company's personnel department and ask for recommendations in each specialty area. Look at directories, such as the *Directory of Executive Recruiters,* issued by *Consultants News,* which lists recruiters by function, specialty, and geography.

Call the recruiters and do your prescreening on the phone. Ask them to describe their background and how they would help in filling your position. The more time spent in prescreening recruiters, the better. If you can, meet with up to six recruiters, with the aim of working with one or more, depending on your needs for special expertise.

Interview recruiters in the same detail you would expect them to quiz you. Check on the length of time they have been in business, whether they consider themselves specialists or generalists, and see whether they have a credible recruiting philosophy.

Do not be afraid to ask how the recruiter would solve your problem. Because she will become one of your confidential consultants and because her work has as long-range an effect on your company as does that of the CPA and attorney, the personal chemistry is important. Talent is necessary, but useless without a good relationship. Certainly you will ask for and check references.

Observe the recruiter's performance during your interview. Evaluate his questions about your firm and the job(s) to be filled. The odds are that the recruiters who ask the most pointed questions are probably the most thorough and will do the best job.

Small companies have to be discerning in their choice of recruiters. There are as many incompetent employment agencies, unprofessional contingency recruiters, and phony executive search firms as in any other field. If you pick a bad firm to work with and the results are bad, it is probably your fault for not using good business judgment.

Fees for recruiters are not determined by regulation, but are competitive. The fee structure of the employment agency and the contingency recruiter is referred to as a percent per thousand—one percentage point in fee for every thousand dollars of salary. So the fee for a $25,000 job would be 25 percent up to a maximum of 30 to 35 percent.

Companies usually charge about the same in one area of the country, but the fees vary by region. In the New York City area, for example, the maximum fees are 35 percent, while they are lower in Philadelphia and Boston and higher in Chicago than in Los Angeles. Another difference in fees can be traced to the ways in which firms invoice: employment agents and contingency recruiters are paid once the job is done, while executive search consultants may be paid the same total amount but on a retainer basis, starting at the time the agency is engaged.

A typical fee arrangement would be one-third of the projected total amount (30 to 35 percent of the estimated compensation of the job) to initiate the work, one-third of the balance after one month, and the balance upon completion. Some firms charge their fee even if the assignment is not completed. Executive search firms tend to charge expenses as well. To avoid unpleasant and unnecessary arguments, be sure to confirm all of the facts concerning fees, expenses, and performance in a letter agreement before starting. If you are unsure of the meaning of any of the provisions, bring in your attorney.

It may be hard to compare the costs of a recruiter with the firm's doing the job itself, because each company's in-house capability is different. Some studies indicate that there is a slight advantage in using a third-party, outside recruiter. The comparison includes not only the hours spent by top people in interviewing and checking references, but advertising, travel, testing, and other out of pocket costs. Harder to measure is the loss to the company of the contribution of the professional, technical, and managerial jobs during the time they are open, what the economist would call opportunity costs.

The comparison should not be limited to costs. Time may be even more important. Generally, recruiters are able to do the job faster than in-house people. They are in the full-time business of maintaining files of qualified people who are actively seeking jobs. They are clearly more experienced in interviewing and checking references than the smaller company manager assigned to the job. In many cases, small firms are unable to come up with the candidates they need through their own devices. This is especially so in fields where the labor market has been tight, such as in engineering, data processing, and key management, and where few people are looking to change their jobs.

Recruiters may help small companies in competing against large firms for good people. Large companies invest heavily in their recruiting, using advertising, glossy brochures, college contacts, and all three types of professional recruiting agencies. Large firms are usually better at the technical aspects of employment, such as job definitions, listing job tasks, and assigning experience and personal criteria to match the job needs.

Smaller companies can afford to be less systematic and formal in these areas, but they are prone to drift into confused and sloppy job criteria. The result is more hiring mistakes. Recruiters can make the first contact with good candidates who are considering both a large and small firm more professional. Good recruiters can help a small company define what it needs in personal, personality, and professional terms. Because it is impossible to hire in a vacuum, careful job definitions are a key responsibility for the recruiter. Professional recruiters can also get smaller company managers to be realistic about the people they are likely to attract for a job.

Assuming they have a small company's approval, recruiters may be capable of approaching competitors or allied companies to attract people.

Successful recruitment requires time on the part of the company's managers. Small companies shortchange themselves by not putting enough time into hiring and by not using all available sources. The recruiter's job is to beat the bushes for the right people, interview and evaluate them, and introduce them to the client for her final hiring decision. Because decisions about staff should be made carefully the interview process should be long. Both recruiters and their smaller firm clients should be prepared to spend hours on interviews and reference checks. Good recruiters check as many as twelve or fifteen references, both professional and personal. They ask enough questions to find consistency in the responses. If the answers are inconsistent, you or the recruiter may want to look back on your interview and see what you can discover.

Reference-checking provides the opportunity to look for other people who might know the candidate. For another, contrary, point of view, you may want to find people who did not hold the candidate in high esteem.

Small company managers who have neither the time nor experience to hire top people or who have no access to candidates with specialty skills should seriously consider picking a professional recruiter with whom they feel at ease. A recruiter can be a valuable outside consultant.

Advertising

How you alert candidates to a job's availability controls the quality of the applicants you attract. These days, almost all private sector recruitment is conducted through published advertising, the quality of which often receives less attention than it should.

Where an ad is placed, how it is displayed, and how it is written control whom it will attract and how much time you will spend in filling the job it advertises. Obviously, job seekers are not going to look for ads in places inappropriate to their line of work or interest. Production workers are not going to look for jobs among the display advertisements of the financial section of the Sunday *New York Times,* nor is a manager qualified to run a $100 million manufacturing operation going to look for a job in the classified pages of any newspaper. Therefore, selecting the advertising medium is the first step in reaching the best qualified candidates.

Two considerations apply in the selection of where to place the ad:

1. The technical level of the job
2. The rarity of the skills involved

The *technical* level of the job determines the readership of ads written for the job. The *rarity* of the skills involved determines the extensiveness of the geographic coverage. The two considerations are guides to selecting the publication(s) in which to advertise.

If the job is an undistinguished one involving mostly common skills, the local paper will usually do. But if the job is highly technical, involving a specialized skill (such as color-matching or knowledge of a specific field, such as international taxation or robot design), you will want to advertise in a publication with the widest readership among the specialists or in a combination of media such as the *Wall Street Journal, New York Times* (Sunday edition), *Los Angeles Times, The Journal of Taxation, Chemical Weekly,* or *National Electronics.*

The location of the ad in a publication, its size, and its use of graphics can greatly influence who will be attracted to it and read it. When we advertise we always ask the advice of the publication's employment advertising consultant about ad location (e.g., right-hand page at top, outside columns), size (e.g., two columns wide, eight inches long), and appearance (e.g., black border, heavy type, medium word density). Where an ad is placed and how it looks are almost as important as the advertising medium itself.

The writing of the ad is the last of the concerns. Here is what we have learned in the writing of hundreds of recruitment ads:

1. Caption the ad to attract the people you really want.
2. Write the ad to cause the readers to screen themselves.
3. Use a blind box number.

The caption of the ad is the trigger to reading the ad. Its importance is directly related to the rarity of the skills of the job; the higher the level or the more specialized the position, the more selective in their reading the candidates are likely to be. Therefore, spend more care in captioning the ad as the importance of the job rises. It is not always necessary to use formal job titles, such as Manager–Quality Control or Vice-President–Finance at the head of the ad. General terms, such as Sales Builder or Developer of Home Protection Devices, can also be used. Amplified to connote something of the scale or nature of the work, the caption can be even more attractive: for example, Traveling Manager of Overseas Sales or Self-Starting Robot Designer. Make the caption as eye-catching as possible. Formal job titles have the least attraction value.

Unless you want to be drowned in a sea of resumes, include door-closers in the ad; that is, include information about the job expectations or the required experience that will turn away the people you do not want. For example, you certainly do not want people who want to work only for large companies and you may not want people who dislike travel or long hours. To keep them from responding, put information in the ad that emphasizes the smallness of the firm, the amount of travel, and long hours involved.

On the other side of the coin, get the best qualified job hunters to respond by including information on the company's growth prospects, plans, and financial condition (facts, not puffery). No worthwhile candidate wants to work for a no-growth, seat-of-the-pants,

---

DIRECTOR POLYMER RESEARCH
Smaller, growing, profitable chemical manufacturer seeks polymer chemist/engineer with experience in polymer reactions, extrusion and characterization, who will grow with us on the way to $50MM in the next 5 years. Top compensation and freedom to use skills and experience in helping us fulfill our planned goals. Emphasis is on industry experience and track record in working with polymers and carrying R&D projects forward through plant production. Will be responsible for managing product development, equipment selection, initial production runs, QC thereafter, and laboratory control. Northern location. Reply by detailed resume to:
X1234 NEWS 56789

Figure 5–1. Sample Employment Ad

financially weak organization, unless it is in a turnaround situation. Good people generally look for employment in companies that have a future, plan for it, and have the means to make it happen.

Figure 5–1 shows an ad we placed for a client within the last year. It is not one of our more spectacular ones, but it illustrates a couple of our points. Note the first word in the text—*Smaller*. That size is mentioned first shows that we were convinced that some polymer chemist/engineers would not want to work in a smaller company and that we did not want resumes from those who would not work for the client company because of its size. Note the mention of the firm's growth prospects, the growth potential of the position, and the degree of initiative to be given the incumbent. Note also that the ad is written to convey an impression of an open, decisive, and sharing management style without advertising it directly

6 ❦
Interviewing Techniques

Interviewing is universally used in recruiting personnel. Because we have all been interviewed and use interviews in so many aspects of our work, we have come to view interviewing as a natural part of personnel and management activity.

But there is a paradox involved in interviewing. Although we lean very heavily on it in recruitment, we really do not know whether it improves the chances of making a good hiring decision. Few investigations of the subject have been made. We know there are flaws in the way most people handle interviews, and our experience tells us that the interviewing skills of most people can be greatly improved.

This chapter deals with ways to improve your interviewing: the questions that should be asked, the things that should be looked for, and the techniques that can be used to improve recruiting results.

The Golden Finger Fallacy

If there is one illusion all managers seem to share, it is thinking they know how to choose a good person. "I know who's going to make it in this company" and "I have a gift for picking the right people" are the sounds of managers possessed by the illusion, which we call the *Golden Finger Fallacy.*

The illusion nullifies interviewing, and when interviewing is the principal means of choosing people, it multiplies the risk of choosing the wrong person. The selection interview, in which one stranger talks to another in a pressured situation about intimate feelings while trying to present his best image to satisfy his economic needs, is difficult enough to make productive. When conducted by a person convinced he possesses "people-picking" gifts, it is almost impossible to make the interview valuable.

Most of us are not born with the inherent ability to interview. Investigation has shown that many interviewers make up their minds about the interviewee in the first five minutes and then spend fifty-five minutes confirming the first impression. Because no one is hired without an interview, we certainly do not propose that the procedure be eliminated. But we do suggest that it be recognized and used as a limited tool and that it be supplemented by other methods that improve the selection process.

The Purposes of Interviewing

What is the purpose of interviewing? Is it to help applicants decide whether the company is the right one for them? Is it to screen people who are likely candidates and select those who will be given further tests before the final selection? Is it to test candidates' abilities to do the job? The purpose is all of these and more. But what takes place in an interview is likely to have a different focus depending on who is doing the interviewing.

Whatever the focus may be, a tendency almost universally shared is to present the firm's good points, not its wants. For recruitment purposes, the traditional practice of making the company a special, exciting, and secure place to work and a leader in its field may seem justified. But, while it may net the firm the outstanding candidate, it also may lay the grounds for losing her. Creating expectations in candidates higher than can be realized after they join the firm is one of the surer ways of seeing to their eventual departure. Studies of voluntary turnover (when the employee leaves of her own accord) show that the traditional recruitment interview is a major source of the disillusionment that follows.

It is hard to strike a balance between selling the organization to a desirable candidate and realistically describing the organization, dark spots and all. But the cost of not presenting a balanced picture can be high. If you hire a person who cannot satisfy his needs on the job, he will leave. If you hire a person who can satisfy his needs in any job, he is likely to be incompetent.

The purpose of recruitment is to match two different sets of characteristics:

1. job requirements with the skills required to fill them
2. environments with the needs and aspirations of individuals who may work in them

Obviously, compromises in demands have to be made on both sides. Well conducted interviews can help determine whether the compromises can be achieved.

Realistic Recruitment

The way to prevent losing people because of their frustration in not being able to get the experience and status they believed was available when they were recruited is realistic recruitment.[1] Realism in recruitment, which is the first casualty to inexperience and subjectivism in interviewing, can be protected or raised in a number of ways. A start is to make clear the purpose of the interview and the way the interview will proceed.

One of the best interviewers we know starts out by saying: "My job in this session is not to judge your qualifications but to tell you all I can about the company and position so you can judge for yourself how you and the job may fit together. After I've finished describing the company and job and answering your questions about them, the next step is for you to say whether you want the job or not. If you say you do, we'll check out your qualifications."

The interviewer then cautions the candidate against saying he wants the job if he knows his qualifications do not match the requirements of the job as described by the interviewer. "You'll just waste a lot of your time if you say you want to go on but the two don't match," warns the interviewer.

The approach accords with two of the fundamental aims of the interview process: to match job needs with the achievements and potentials of applicants and to screen out people who are simply looking for any job. An example of the latter is the case of the phone-screening interview for a position as vice-president of engineering and manufacturing in a $6-million-a-year company, which was to pay

---

[1]Well described in *Organizational Entry* by John P. Wanous, Reading, Mass.: Addison-Wesley Publishing Company, 1980.

about $50,000. One of the resumes was from the president of a division of a large company whose sales were $100 million and whose base salary was $85,000. It was clear that the status, opportunity for growth, and in-house resources to do the job, as well as the financial needs of the applicant, would not be filled. If he took the job, it would be only as an interim stop while he looked for something else to put him back in the job and salary league in which he properly felt he should be.

Traditionally, the interview has been used both as a recruitment device, to attract candidates, and as a selection tool, to choose from among the attracted those who will be offered a position. Neither purpose is inherently sensitive to the personal and private reasons a candidate is interested in the job. It is up to you as interviewer to seek out the reasons a person is looking for a job of the kind advertised and in your kind of organization and to determine whether she will be able to satisfy the needs of the job and the organization and be happy in both. Probing an individual's interests will not reduce your chances of hiring her, but lack of probing is almost certain to reduce the probability of her being successful on the job.

Since the most dependable measure of selection is not that the candidate will be happy in the job but rather that she can do the job, we look to the interview to find out the applicant's achievements—what she did before—and her potential—what she is likely to be able to do. The key question then becomes, is the interview the best way to do both?

Another technique of realistic recruitment is to include direct questions about the way the candidate perceives and would manage the job. For example, what do you think a job here will mean to you? How long do you think it will take you to learn the job and become contributory? How fast do you think you will reach $_____ salary? How long do you think it will take you to prepare yourself to move to the next level in the organization? How much of your time do you think you will be spending with people, on the phone, in meetings, following orders, having freedom to do what you want? How many outside training sessions will you want to attend, and why? How much travel and overtime do you think the job requires? Answers to such questions have at least two values. First, they reveal a good deal about a candidate's confidence in his ability to do the job and about his interpersonal competence. Second, honest answers require an openness which introduces risks only strong candidates are willing to undertake.

Most people do not read or remember the information presented in a company brochure. Eliciting the questions or asking people what they think will happen to them in their daily work and their job progress in the interview, as described on the previous page, is a good way to get the truth across.

It is sometimes fruitful to have candidates spend time with people on the job. The prospective employee reasonably concludes that the sample of work he experiences is representative. The truth, of course, is usually different. The sample is likely to be nonrepresentative. It was probably chosen to represent the best part of the job, or the person with whom the applicant speaks is picked because of his commitment to the company and his warmth and enthusiasm. Therefore, realistic recruitment provides opportunities for editorial comments and feedback after the job exposure. "Tell me your impressions of what you just did or saw and how they relate to what you might do if you came to work here." The resulting feedback gives the interviewer an opportunity to correct any false impressions.

ACHIEVEMENTS VERSUS POTENTIAL

It is easier to obtain information about achievements than to judge potential. We have frequently urged clients to hire people who have done things that can be checked rather than to take the chance of hiring people who may be able to do things in the future, but who have only shown hints of what they may become. In large organizations, able to make the investment in hiring many people and training, screening, and losing most, hiring potential makes sense. However, the smaller company can less well afford the high attrition involved in developing people from potential to achievement, and has, accordingly, less experience in development. The competitive pressure felt by smaller companies is usually from companies as small or smaller, most of which do not have to factor high personal development costs into their pricing.

Emphasizing achievement has other practical benefits. If the candidate has done the work for which he is recruited, he can be quizzed in detail and put through role-playing or simulated problem situations in which the currency and extent of his knowledge can be evaluated. He can be interviewed by outside experts or knowledgeable in-house peers (who cannot otherwise measure his abilities), and, above all, factual evidence of how well he did the work in the past can be checked.

Compare this approach with the difficulty of measuring potential. Getting high grades in school is probably best as an indicator of getting high grades in school in the future. But, it is a poor predictor of job success. Your conclusion about the way a candidate will work out, even after several interviews, will be lucky to be 50 percent accurate in the absence of information about past performance in a job similar to the one for which she is being interviewed. Assessment centers that put candidates in situations comparable to those of the job are beyond the reach of most smaller companies, which are left with interviewing, psychological testing, reference checking, and, where possible, probationary periods on the job. Although each of these techniques is useful when properly employed, none is as dependable a predictor of success in a new job as is previous success in a similar job.

Certainly, we do not suggest that smaller companies limit hiring to people with selected experience. That could be as damaging as selecting only on potential. Every firm that has grown beyond the entrepreneur(s) that built it needs infusions of fresh blood to avoid becoming a captive of its own narrow experience. But, on the whole, smaller companies should choose new people on the basis of demonstrated skill in the jobs for which they are being hired.

Wanous points out that studies show that introducing realistic recruitment does not reduce success in hiring.[2] When and how to be realistic have also been studied. Since each applicant brings his own expectations to the interview, it is clearly best to get the truth out as soon as possible. One way to do this is in printed brochures. The telephone company had a significant decrease in turnover when it described the operator's job in non-glamorous terms in the brochure sent to interested applicants. A law firm interviewed young lawyers three and six months after they were hired (at salaries reported as astronomical in the business press) and found that the part of the job that was most upsetting, and of which the young lawyers had been ignorant, was the time required. True, they were earning $30 to $40 thousand, but they were working sixty to seventy-five hours a week, which brought their hourly pay down to levels comparable with those of other graduate professionals.

DESCRIBE JOB OPPORTUNITIES REALISTICALLY

Of all the steps that can be taken toward realistic recruitment, none has more importance than telling the truth.

The perfect illustration is the prospect of ownership. Opportunities for stock ownership are a sensitive concern in family-held or closely held firms. Bringing in outsiders is seen as making the shareholder a partner and vastly complicating life. Children lurk in the background, often ten or fifteen years from reasonable expectations of being managers. The father still wants to make sure that nothing upsets the possibility of his child being the sole owner or majority

---

[2]*Organizational Entry.*

controller of the company. The new manager asks the standard question: "What's the chance of my becoming a stockholder, by purchase or receipt of a stock bonus?" Being realistic, the question is valid and pertinent to hiring good candidates. It can be answered this way: "We have no intention of making shares available to anyone except family members at this time. However, we will work out with you a compensation program that will permit you to share in the earnings and increased value of the company based on your contribution. Performance shares, some type of non-voting stock, or an individual deferred compensation plan are possibilities."

In addition, realistic expectations of career opportunities should be fostered. The expectations should be directed toward actual or foreseeable family competition and the company's rate of growth. If family members are likely to be moving into management positions, the place on the organizational chart available or expected to be available to the incoming manager should be made clear. The consequence of not doing this is attracting people who do not care about their future—maintenance and security seekers—rather than tigers and achievers.

Being realistic about corporate growth is tougher. Many small companies have no plans, or only vague ones, for the future. The age of the owner may have a significant influence on whether the company will grow: at some point many people decide they want to hold on to what they have accumulated and do not want to take additional risks. Hiring a person who can handle what you have is an appropriate selection policy. But it should be made clear to the new person that you are more interested in retaining than growing. Obviously, a specific type of person will be attracted and will stay under this condition.

A retail chain was owned and run by a sixty-two-year-old man whose twenty-seven-year-old son decided to enter the family business after five years as a product manager with Procter & Gamble. The father was immensely proud of the independent success his son had achieved in P & G, but was also realistic enough to know that his son would need help in finance and probably in manufacturing, areas for which the father had been responsible. The son's marketing background was stronger than that of anyone in the company. The father decided to support his son by bringing in experienced outside executives in each function. The selection process aimed at finding two good people who were willing to act as counselors, would accept the fact that they would not become CEO unless the son was no longer in the company, and would get their satisfaction from guiding the son and, in time, training their own successors. These criteria determined that the jobs should be filled by middle-aged men who had made peace with their professional aspirations, knew they would never get rich nor become shareholders, but would be guaranteed security and a special satisfaction if they did their job well.

The recruitment interviews made crystal clear what the jobs would *not* provide: no stock, no CEO opportunity, but ten to fifteen years' security and a chance to participate in the company's growth through individual deferred compensation plans based on company earnings.

Another example of realistic recruitment took place in the case of a small retail chain which developed a plan for fast expansion. The CEO had four family members in the business with three in the wings ready to join as soon as they were educated. What was lacking among the family members was someone with experience in acquisitions and negotiations. The company's growth plan was based on a wide canvassing of smaller stores in the area, and then applying one of three basic acquisition formulas, each modifiable to satisfy the individual needs of the seller. The recruitment interview made clear that the job was a two to three year position. The owner assumed that a capable person would probably have brought in the digestible number of acquisitions within the period and would not be interested in or capable of running the acquired companies. Further, family members were slotted for those jobs. The skill of the acquisition manager was that of a sales representative: achieving success through the making of deals. Operating the acquired business required a less achieving type of person, one with more modest aspirations and the ability to handle continued relationships with store managers.

The problem was how to hire someone for only two or three years. Don't most people want at least the prospect of a longer job? Most do, but not all. Look upon the negotiator or acquirer as a professional who wants to add to his list of professional scalps ten to fifteen acquisitions made for a small retail chain; who sees the job not only as an opportunity to add to his experience and value to his next employer but also as a means of making big money for the two or three years; and who wants to be exposed to opportunities to get into business for himself.

In this case, the compensation program included a bonus for every successful deal, approved by the owner and the outside CPA and attorney, and the right of the acquirer-negotiator to negotiate for any deal the company turned down six months after he left them.

Implied in these last two examples is a personnel philosophy we mentioned in our book, *Survival & Growth: Management Strategies for the Small Firm* (AMACOM 1974). The smaller company should hire for need, not for life. Particularly in areas of specialization, when a younger person needs counselling, or when you have a problem that requires a few years to straighten out and that can then be left to a new, younger manager, look to hiring an older person or professional of any age who only wants a short-term involvement.

The Interview Process

OPEN-ENDED QUESTIONS

One of the beauties of open-ended interviewing is that you do not have the moral limitations of setting up traps; you do not screen people with shrewd questioning or subtleties only able to be designed by a trained psychologist; all you do is ask people to sell themselves by describing their strengths to satisfy their self-image.

What to ask in an interview is critical: we start with an awareness of the limitations of the interview process. Its main purpose is to determine the applicant's achievements and skills in relation to the job needs and to determine her interests, needs, and expectations, so that if she is hired, the job has a reasonable chance of satisfying her. A good fit should be made by both parties.

A quotation may bring the necessary humility to the interview process: "The basic difficulty of this type of interview, as usually conducted, is that it involves making extensive inferences from limited data obtained in artificial situations by unqualified observers."[3] We want to reduce errors by explaining the mechanics of a good selection interview. Most of us are not born as expert interviewers. But the skills *can* be learned.

Both careful interview techniques and structured interviews are helpful in improving the process and results. If someone is going to interview a great deal, he should take a short course, read several good books on the subject, such as *Interviewing for Managers*, John D. Drake, AMACOM 1972 and *Practical Interviewing*, Glenn A. Bassett, AMACOM 1965, and submit to a videotape replay of his handling an interview. If this replay is analyzed by a professional interviewer, interviewing skill can be improved.

STRUCTURED INTERVIEW QUESTIONS

To develop comparability between applicants, conduct structured interviews in which you ask all applicants the same questions in the

[3]M. M. Mandell, "The Group Oral Performance Test," *Personnel Administration* 15, no. 6 (1951):2.

same sequence. Following are samples of questions from a structured interview:[4]

> First, some general rules. Your job is primarily to listen. You should speak only to get more information or to provide answers to specific questions. A good ratio between your listening and talking is 80–20.
>
> Listening is an active not a passive function in interviewing. You listen not only for the words but for the emotional content, the hesitations, the enthusiasms, the body language, the eye contact. This means you have to be responsive. When something doesn't add up in your experience or seems incomplete or contradictory, immediately delve and explore: "I don't understand" or "Could you give me an example of that?" or "How else might you have handled that?" or "With hindsight, what do you think you learned from that?" or "That doesn't seem to tie in with—you mentioned before. Could you explain the point in another way?"
>
> Look for details. Start listening with the end product in mind—you want to make a decision on whether someone is fit to handle a specific job in your company's environment. You want specific evidence to back that decision. Assume you were the candidate's attorney and had to plead a case for him with a skeptical outsider. This would require hard facts more than impressions, which are hard to defend. Get as many facts and as much auditable evidence as you can.
>
> Look for appearance, dress, manner, ability to express, listen, and respond. These are impressions, true, but we all make evaluations of people's skills or appearance in these areas. Be alert to your own prejudices. If you are an athlete and the small talk with which you start to break the ice deals with sports, be conscious of your own bias in favor of the person who immediately picks up the opening and carries on an enthusiastic and knowledgeable sports talk with you. Just as clearly, don't hold it against someone because he's bored with sports and has nothing to say about your favorite activity. Dress and manner may be important *if the job requirements include special criteria in those areas.* But if the job can be filled by someone of any size, looks, dress, background but acceptable level of competence, don't get side-tracked by an applicant's obvious charm or well-presented superficial appearance.
>
> Consider the variety of sizes, shapes, ages, backgrounds, looks, and any other personal factor you can list in successful sales people. There is *no* single sales appearance or manner that is uniformly successful. There *is* a pattern of personality traits, interests, achievement need, and other skills in successful salesmen (*see* "What Makes a Good Salesman," by David Mayer and Herbert M. Greenberg, *Harvard Business Review,* July–August, 1964).
>
> Questions to ask about work experience—full, part-time, military:
>
> What have you done best—what do you think the success shows about you as a person? (Be relentless in pursuing this question—what did the person do best? It provides one of the most consistent patterns of work behavior. Trace the "best" experiences back as far in the work history as possible.)

[4]*Staffing Policies and Strategies,* edited by Dale Yoder and Herbert G. Heneman, Jr., Washington, D.C.: The Bureau of National Affairs, Inc., pages 4, 150, 152.

What have you done less than well? Why?

What have you liked to do? What parts of your work have been least satisfying? Why?

If you were to write your own obituary or eulogy, for what experiences or achievements in all your work history would you like to be remembered? (Since most people don't plan their eulogies, this question helps to identify the strongest self-image feelings a candidate has—the strengths for which you may be interested in hiring him.)

What were the most difficult problems you've had to face? How did you handle them? How would you handle them today?

What are the most effective techniques you have found in dealing with people? (Start with the open-ended question, then follow up more specifically: how did you handle supervisory problems, your peers, your boss, annoying customers or suppliers?)

How much did you earn—base, bonus and special fringe benefits? Was the pay fair for what you did? If not, what should it have been? What did you do when you felt your pay was not right? (The level of self-confidence, self-image and aggressiveness *may* be shown in answers to these questions. To some people money is a major symbol of who they are.)

Why did you leave jobs? (Follow up to get facts if you can. This is only one area where reference checking often reveals more than one version of the "truth.")

What are you looking for in a work career—for the next 3, 5, or more years? Why do you say what you did?

What earnings do you expect in the next 3, 5, 10 years and how do you justify the amounts? (These last two questions are good indications of maturity and reality.)

GET SPECIFICS

In this series of questions on work experience look for signs of the relevance of what the person did to the job you are trying to fill. Get *specifics*. It is amazing how many people were solely responsible for growth and profits and had nothing to do with losses. If the applicant says she did something (increased sales, developed products, cut costs, installed a cost system or computer, hired, acquired, financed, anything), ask her who else was involved—at the same level, above, and below. Ask whether her boss and her subordinates would give her the same credit. Or, who else should have been given credit. Team players say "we" while soloists prefer "I."

Education history may be important, but we are skeptical of grades and school experiences because of the almost random relationship between good school grades and business success. Also, students mature at different ages. We all know late-blooming children who did not realize what school was until they were out of it, but who have done extraordinarily well at work. School experiences can be relevant if education requirements are critical and because school *is* a part of life in offering opportunities for leadership, initiative, and self-dependence, and in revealing motivation and interests.

Ask about best and most difficult subjects; extracurricular activities; reasons for choosing major subject; if the person has worked, the relevance of his education to his career; what he would have preferred to study if he could do it again; how did he finance his education—if he did it himself, how does he feel about the time and effort required compared to those students whose parents paid their way?

Interviewers vary in their questioning about early years: family relationships, attitudes about parents, siblings, and social background. Our feeling is that exploration of this area may be valuable more for the applicant's comments and insight than the facts themselves. We prefer to omit family questions, but to be alert to family and background references and to ask for observations when the applicant brings up the subject.

OUTSIDE INTERESTS

Current interests and activities outside of work are useful areas to explore. Be sure to avoid any questions on race, religion, or politics for obvious nondiscriminatory reasons. But ask questions dealing with:

Special hobbies and interests (not just the listing, but how much time does the person spend; if athletics, how good is he—sometimes an indication of self-discipline).

Ask about the present family—number and age of children. The spouse's work situation may be important.

Aside from hobbies, sports, and family, what does the person do in his spare time? (The answers tell whether the applicant has broad or narrow interests, whether his cultural and intellectual demands are likely to be satisfied in his work, whether he will fit into the working environment, whether he has been recognized as a leader in social, political, or other groups—all useful pieces to build up a picture.)

If location and travel are part of the job, get the applicant's feelings or limitations out in the open soon.

Hardest of all, since most of us do not think through the question and are reluctant to share our feelings with strangers, try to determine from answers and questions what the applicant's basic values are. Sometimes, asking for the toughest decisions the applicant ever had to make, aside from purely personal ones, reveals what the person feels is important. As many philosophers have said: The tough choice is between two goods or two bads. If the applicant describes such a choice and you explore why it was a hard decision, you may have a real insight into his basic values.

Summarize the interview by giving the applicant a chance to make sure you understood her and are considering her in the proper, most accurate light. Ask what she will bring to the job; what her strengths, weaknesses, and concerns are? What training or experience might she need to be more productive? Why does she feel the company is the place for her? Encourage any last questions or comments she wants the interviewer to have.

SUMMARIZE

Finally, to put everything together, write down your findings immediately after the interview. We prefer to take notes (and tell the applicant we are doing so in order not to miss anything) during the interview. Indicate the major strengths and weaknesses in relation to the job. List what she will bring to the job and to the company.

What else do you have to know? What are you going to check in the references? What experts or outsiders should meet the person to explore further areas of special concern? Who else in the company should he meet?

OTHER CONSIDERATIONS

The physical setup of the interview is important for both the mechanics of privacy and the symbolic importance you place on the interview. There should be *no* interruptions except for real emergencies. Offer coffee or a soft drink; if the interview is at mealtime, you add a gracious note by eating out at a pleasant, quiet restaurant or by having a sandwich or salad lunch in your office.

Do your homework by reading the resume and making notes of things on which you want to follow up. The resume is an excellent place to start the interview, since all applicants commonly assume you will have some questions. Or, start the meeting with small talk; the applicant is probably nervous. Ask him about his trip to the office, parking, the weather, or any immediate current event.

Take time. You will feel more secure in making the hiring decision (and so will the applicant in making the decision to come to work) if you plan to spend a minimum of an hour and one-half. Do not pressure for answers. If the applicant seems to be struggling, note it, then come back when she is more relaxed and you know better how to ask the question.

At the end of the interview tell the applicant what his chances are and *why*. Tell him what you think his strengths are and where you have doubts. If he is a strong candidate and seems interested, tell him what the next step is. We think that honest recruiting includes a reasonable expectation of some commitment of at least interest from the applicant. If you are interested, ask for references at this time, if you have not written them down in the course of the interview. Be sure you are clear as to which ones you can call. We will have more to say about reference-checking.

Group Interviews

The key management in a small company often acts as a partnership. Compatability may be as important as competence. We often suggest that new top managers or technical people who will be dealing with top management be interviewed by the whole management group. To avoid the time of sequential interviewing, consider organized group interviews.

The best candidates who have been screened, reference-checked, and tested, where applicable, are scheduled to meet the top group in sixty to ninety minute sessions. Because it is hard for a candidate to deal with five or six questioners simultaneously, one person is selected to be chief questioner. Using a standard, agreed-upon interview format for comparability, the chief questioner conducts the first 75 percent of the interview while the others listen. For the balance of the time, the floor is open to questions from everyone.

Immediately upon completing a group interview, before the next candidate is invited into the room, the group lists the strengths and weaknesses of each candidate. By the end of the day you will have identified the two or three best people and what you as a group like and do not like about each of them. Invite the top candidates back for a final interview, telling them in advance on which strengths and weaknesses you want to focus. You should be able to make a decision with the benefit of every important manager's opinion and reduce the error factor to a practical minimum.

Of all the characteristics you must seek in a manager, none is more important than integrity. Integrity cannot be taught; it is inherent in the value system of each of us by the time we go to work, certainly by the time we are ready to be considered for management responsibility. Because the small company management team rarely consists of more than a dozen people, more often five or six, the message of what is important not only in personnel policies but in dealing with customers, vendors, professionals, and the community is shown by whom you hire, reward, and promote to the top management group.

Look for Integrity

When it comes to integrity, people cannot be fooled. It is unfair to employees to be supervised by someone who lacks integrity because he is working for his own interests—subordinates have to protect themselves and cannot work for the company. Employees do not respect a top management that permits the wrong people to remain in responsible jobs or that rewards the wrong behavior. In one company, the dismissal of a relative who had been stealing; in another company, the buying out of an uncle who had been grossly overpaid; in a third company, the decent handling of a sixty-three-year-old employee with forty years' longevity by putting him in a position where he could not hurt the firm were all greeted by others in the organization as signs that management respected the integrity of personnel relationships as much as the obligations of blood or years.

The last statement is not meant to suggest that you disregard long years. If someone is no longer able to handle his job because he or it has changed, you, the manager-owner, are responsible for having let the condition reach the state that it now requires action. Your message as to integrity is clear in how you correct the historical error: do what the company needs *and* consider the individual.

Seeking integrity is hard in selecting applicants from the outside. In most small companies, you know the potential managers and have seen them in a variety of situations. We had a pleasant experience with one owner who made a point of putting his key people, particularly the younger ones, in positions where they had to make difficult decisions: telling or not telling customers the truth about marginal quality; using personal information in dealing with union leaders; sharing with competitors information, which might be considered collusive or merely professional.

In making the decision to promote someone or to hire an outsider, where the facts are considerably fewer, you may find it helpful to use standards we applied in deciding whether a candidate was fit to be a partner.

Does the applicant have the technical knowledge for the job? (You would rarely consider someone without this basic skill.)

Was he treated as a partner (manager) by those he dealt with *before* he was given the title? (This is a good test because it assumes, rightly, that most people cannot be fooled.)

Has he made the right decisions when he has had a tough choice? (If he has not had the opportunity, what does your inside, intestinal reaction say he would do? Trust your intuitive feeling—it is rarely wrong, particularly in answering this question.)

Finally, if you were to introduce the person as "my partner" or "my vice-president" how would you feel (proud, not excited, or mumbling and ashamed)? (This is another way of testing your total impression of the person.)

PERSONALITY TYPES AS SELECTION CRITERIA

Classifying candidates into types and allowing the classification to factor in selection decisions is commonplace and properly subject to criticism. Candidates are individuals, and a correctly conducted interview is an attempt to discover those aspects of a person's nature appropriate to the job. Too often, personal characteristics get in the way and divert the interviewer. However, it is also true that people tend to fall into recognizable categories, and that fact can be used to direct your interview toward its recruitment objectives.

The star whose price to attract or retain is almost irrelevant because of his value to you will come across your path only a few times in your life. Such a person has the sensitivity through intuition and experience to create, inspire, and mold an organization through his passion and competence. Such a person is usually capable of simultaneously juggling a variety of tasks and doing them all well. His energy and confidence and his ability to be ahead of the group may have gotten him into trouble. In interviewing him, you may feel that he cannot wait to get his hands on *your* job because he knows he can do it better than you can.

Such a person may be hard to handle. He is probably abrasive, cocksure, impatient, and intimidates others with his energy and confidence. This star is probably trying to beat a parent or sibling, his social background, or his own constant and impossibly difficult expectations.

If you can see through the difficult facade, consider hiring such a person on a tough contingency basis. Agree on high but achievable standards that can be met only if the person works hard under constant pressure. Offer mouth-watering rewards if he succeeds, termination if he fails.

A second type of candidate is the professional bureaucrat who rises by seniority, neatness, and providing order and security to others. She likes the power and position of her job, and enjoys getting others to follow orders. She is useful in making order out of a mess and in maintaining an existing organization. But do not look for risk-taking or initiative beyond the cosmetic and reactive from her.

A third group of managers (and often salespeople) includes the talker, persuader, and charmer, whose sole interest is in selling himself. He makes a poor executive but a good salesperson. This type of candidate can create empathy by using first names sooner than you may feel comfortable; makes it clear that he likes and wants to be liked; probably talks well; and is sensitive to status, money, and recognition.

Selling is probably the only place for such a person. It offers money-making opportunities directly proportionate to his efforts; it can be dignified as a profession; and it can be interpreted as helping others.

The final character is the actor, the person who goes through the motions of being an executive but who rarely produces results. She is charming, often smooth and pleasant, and in early stages of acquaintance usually impressive. A test for this type of person is to try to summarize what an actor said, pleasant and intelligent-sounding as her words might have been. The analysis will show little. The actor's verbal skills exceed her general intelligence. Asked to contribute to a solution, she will make noises but produce nothing upon which the firm can act.

Typically, the actor stays on a job for only a short period. His personal life is also often unstable. His resume has to be checked with care because it is likely to include fictitious jobs, titles, degrees, and even names.

The foregoing gallery of managerial types is not complete, nor would we presume to try to make it so. If anything, the four examples we give are demonstrations of what we take to be a fundamental principle—that people, like organizations, are systems and that systems do not have pieces out of synchrony with the whole.

The principle has great application in interviewing. It rescues the interviewer from the problem of trying to see any candidate in depth. Seeing certain characteristics enables the interviewer to infer with high probability other traits that fit or do not fit the specifications of a job.

In *Secrets of a Corporate Headhunter* (Atheneum, 1980), John Wareham offers a useful list of characteristics and behavior to look for in an interview.

1. Because the interview is a focused, intensive, on-stage experience, the applicant should act with a clear understanding of its importance. It is not a casual social contact.

2. Try to detect signs of energy. Although lazy people say they pick their spots to use their limited energy and, therefore, get more output for their input than ordinary people, you generally will be safer looking for the person with high energy who can stay with any job or problem and see it through.

3. Energy devoted to hobbies, community work, and the family may offer personal satisfaction, but it is not very useful to the firm. You want energy devoted to work. Some evidence of a work ethic are parents or an early boss who made work important and part-time or hobby interests which are activity-oriented rather than passive. For example: the candidate plays an instrument rather than just listens to music; he participates in sports rather than just watches; he builds rather than buys furniture. Other signs of a work-oriented person are a non-clock-watching work schedule, good health (few absences from work), frugality (he lives on 75 percent of his earnings), and high career goals in both position and financial terms.

4. Family background may be revealing. The children of fathers who were entrepreneurs or earned high status jobs, and the oldest of several children are slightly more likely to be successful and responsible than others. Siblings' jobs and successes; number of marriages; spouse's education and occupation; what she expects of her children—all reveal characteristics or a background which may indicate a results and success orientation.

5. Emotional maturity permits a candidate to devote his efforts to his work with minimum interference from internal conflicts. One of the reasons given for Franklin D. Roosevelt's success was his inner balance. He approached problems with minimum diversion from psychological hang-ups. Some signs of a candidate's emotional maturity are the absence of childish, dependent charm; a concern for other people; his major life values and goals; why he chose his jobs and why he left them; how he describes his former bosses. Healthy people usually admit that there are more versions of the truth than their own.

6. Effective managers channel most of their hostilities to the beating of competitors or improving products and profits. The outstanding manager is rarely all sweetness and light. Her drive and ambition may make her abrasive, but she is sensitive enough to know her effect on others, tempers her outbursts, and apologizes and clears the air when necessary, but never at the expense of focusing on the goals.

7. Perseverance is the rarest of managerial capacities. Ideas are

cheap and available everywhere. Look for the manager who has gotten things done. Brilliance is no substitute for effectiveness. The effective manager knows that, and knows how to use the brilliance of others. The reverse is not necessarily true. The outstanding candidate is aware of that and, when asked to describe what he does best, is less likely to say, "management of people, inspiring others, solving problems, being creative, or being a good team member" than "I get things done."

8. Look for solid, clear reasons for his wanting the job in your company. In addition to skill, ambition, and determination, there has to be a fit between what he wants in practical terms and what the company can offer. Do not undervalue such mundane reasons as liking the firm's line of business, geographic location, or style of management. If the gap is too wide, suggest he look elsewhere.

9. Loyalty and constancy to the firm's values and causes are critical to a candidate fitting into a team. That does not mean you want quick yea-sayers. You need people who will agree with your basic aims and standards, feel comfortable in pointing out when you are going off target, but once the decision is made will not sulk and look for revenge, but will join the team. A typical question in this area is, "How did you handle the situation when something you felt strongly about was vetoed?"

10. Look for compatibility. This not only means that you trust your feelings, it means that the firm needs a balance of skills, teamworkers, and age. Too many tigers, too many young, too many technical people, or too many idea people are probably as dangerous as too few.

11. Remember that of the large number of job candidates interviewed, ninety to ninety-five percent will be turned down. Many will rank almost as high as the ones you selected. Even though they have been rejected, applicants who have been treated properly can become goodwill ambassadors for your company. They should be able to talk about the interview and your company hiring standards so positively that other desirable applicants will apply.

A contractor puts every technical and managerial job candidate through four interviews, a three-hour session with an independent consulting psychologist, and a day on the job with three or four employees. If he passes this tough screening, the new employee starts work feeling that he is superior and the company is special. Turnover is ten percent of the industry average and employees are a major source of referrals of new people. When candidates rejected by the contractor compare the firm's high standards and careful selection process with those of the average company, they become public relations ambassadors to the general public, and increase the possibility outstanding people will apply for jobs.

7

Compensation

Pay is a fascinating, if at times baffling, subject. For years we have arrived at answers, through experience, reasoning, or research, only to have them undone not long afterward. But one of our conclusions has never changed; questions of pay can make payers and payees upset faster and longer than can almost any other question of employment.

We have been up to our necks in questions of pay over the years, and in this chapter we would like to share the outcomes of our experiences with you.

Pay as a Resource

Pay is a key management tool. Used improperly it forces managers to eke out results by sweat and stress; used properly, it multiplies the benefits of managers' efforts. Of all the tools of management, none bears more critically upon performance than does pay.

Because it is seen as simple to use and is subject to a great deal of bias, pay lends itself readily to improper usage. Have you ever tried to dig a ditch with only a spade or pry out a nail with a screwdriver?

If you have, you soon leaned how tough it is to work with the wrong tool! Pay, too, has its applications, the kinds of work it can do with great facility. But it cannot do everything asked of it. It is often applied inappropriately.

The conditions under which pay will function as we wish it to are limited. To understand those conditions, we have to look at pay from the perspective of its ultimate purpose: to manage behavior. To some, that will seem coldly manipulative. But if it is, so is all of management, which achieves its assigned results through employing resources—whatever their natures—at the upper levels of their performance capabilities.

As long as the objective in using pay to manage behavior is not limited to parochial interests, such as those of ownership, a family, or top executives, no stigma or handicap attaches to using it so. Furthermore, human personality itself prevents pay from being used successfully to manipulate behavior for narrow purposes.

The conditions under which pay can operate as a motivator are quite precise: they do not include self-serving objectives or results that cannot be traced to individual effort. Where the conditions do not exist, pay either fails to motivate or demotivates. On the other hand, when used in accordance with the proper conditions, pay can achieve much of what we want from it.

Pay, for most people, is important under three conditions:

1. when it is the difference between merely surviving and living decently
2. when it separates top-notch from run-of-the-mill performers
3. when it earns social recognition

Effective compensation planning takes into account and responds to each of the conditions.

Take the first objective—to provide a decent living. On the face of it, the notion seems absurd. Pay continues to be important long after it provides a decent living. After all, the more one gets, the more one wants. Right? Wrong! True, effective managers (along with everybody else) want enough money that they need not scrounge for basic amenities. But, after that, for most of them, money becomes more valuable as a measure of their worth, in their *and* in others' eyes, than for itself. Those who work almost exclusively for money itself are either not receiving as much as they really need or are in the grip of needs no amount of money can satisfy. Therefore, compensation planning should not be concerned with money alone, but with money as a means by which employees can earn self-esteem (the second objective) and social recognition within and outside the organization (the third objective). That requires planning that allows enough satisfaction with salaries that nonmonetary motives can come to the fore.

Three facts control what can and cannot be done with compensation.

Fact 1. A company functions because people will exchange their time, knowledge, skills, and efforts for money and the intangible rewards they consider worthwhile. There is an implied contract between a company and its employees covering what the employees will give in exchange for what they are paid. When employees perceive they are not being paid fairly, they will give less than their best. When employees perceive the primary limits to pay lie within themselves, employees convinced of their worth will give all they can. Since the employee is the discretionary, flexible partner in the psychological contract, and pay more often than not reduces the employee's feeling of equity, management must be sensitive to the *employee's* perception of the work contract.

What keeps you in business and determines your profits is the depth of the resources on which employees are willing to draw. If building family wealth, employing family incompetents at high salaries, or buying competence as cheaply as you can are put ahead of paying people fairly and in accordance with their skills and contribution, your employees will know it and give you only their time, withholding their knowledge and energy. When pay is inadequate for unacceptable reasons, employees will spend a significant portion of their skills and efforts deceiving you, or will leave you for better rewards.

Fact 2. The quality of pay bears materially on organizational structure and size. A lean and smoothly functioning organization is possible only when pay is used to stimulate pride in one's initiative and team spirit. A lean organization, one which is relatively small for the amount of business it does, is always preferable to a fat one with its excessive task specialization, numbers of employees, layers of supervision, and controls. Defective compensation systems are almost always a feature of fat organizations.

Companies that do not use pay to focus employees' efforts on the firm's objectives must use more to accomplish less. Compared to companies that are skillful in the art of compensation, they will watch employees more closely, check on progress more frequently, and rely on elaborate procedures to see that initiative, flexibility, and customer service do not wither and die. That means *more* people than are needed to do the essential work!

Fact 3. Compensation programs are instruments of competition. The effects of pay inevitably show up in the marketplace. An effective program can attract and keep sharp managers and cause them to search for and exploit every opportunity to improve their company's affairs. An ineffective program retains incompetent managers, creates confusion as to what they should spend their time on, fosters organizational conflict and counterproductive behavior, and detracts from the firm's performance in the marketplace. Poor quality, follow-through, and customer relations are among the hallmarks of companies staffed by people either unhappy with or unmotivated by their pay.

Types of Pay

Pay means different things to different people. Pay is what an employee thinks it is. If he defines it as his net weekly paycheck, that's what it is. If it includes fringe benefits, and he is aware of them, that's his pay. And, if it includes some qualitative aspects of the job—such as challenge, working conditions, relationship with his boss, friendships, pride in the company—they, too, are part of his pay. Therefore, to the extent that an employee does not recognize or is unclear about the elements of his pay, it misses its mark, which is to drive performance upward.

Pay comes in five basic forms: base pay, benefits, perquisites, bonuses, and capital accumulation. It is important to see each of them for its differences since each type serves different needs and is viewed differently by those receiving or hoping to receive it.

SALARY OR BASE PAY

Salary is the amount regularly paid for doing a good, or standard, job. In amount, it is usually close to the market value of the job, that is, the amount paid for equivalent jobs by other firms in the same geographic area. For most managers (about 75 percent, according to several studies), salary is the key factor in their total pay.

Dissatisfaction with base pay in firms that pay at least competitive wages seldom causes employees to stay or leave by itself. Salary is only one factor in job satisfaction. Dissatisfaction with pay is often offset by equally powerful influences: the company's prospects, power held, friends, convenience of commuting, alternative options, and so forth.

Nevertheless, our experience suggests the wisdom of being generous in setting base salaries. Salaries that do not meet the basic living needs of employees or meet the needs of employees' standards of living do not free them sufficiently from financial concerns to focus on the firm's interests. Base pay usually falls between 50 and 80 percent of the total compensation package.

Even when generous, salaries themselves are seldom motivating. Most employees think they are the prices that must be paid for their time and services. Progressive companies recognize that fact and resort to other forms of compensation to stimulate extraordinary performance.

BENEFITS

Benefits are the fixed-cost portion of pay, and include the coverages aimed at keeping employees from being diverted by worry about security. Benefits seldom are linked to performance, although some, such as medical-surgical and life insurance, increase with rises in salary and job levels.

Benefits today are so common that they are regarded as necessities and due. Because of the competitive disadvantage a company would face if it tried to attract or retain good people without benefits, it has little choice but to include them. They are, therefore, largely non-motivating. Differences in benefits hardly ever cause movement from one company to another.

Purely in financial terms, benefits deserve attention. Their costs rarely run below 35 percent of base salary and can easily reach 50 percent.

Following is a list of what might be called the necessary benefits:

Medical, surgical, and major medical insurance

Group and other life insurance coverages

Medical reimbursement plans

Vacations (an individualized benefit when offered as an alternative to higher pay or to reward special performance)

Travel and accident insurance (twenty-four-hour coverage)

Professional dues, meetings, and publications

Profit-sharing and pension plans (primarily useful for retention— the contribution of each individual to the corporate results, which affect the amounts set aside, is usually small and the payoff is distant, which reduce the motivational value of the plans)

Medical examinations (they may confirm management's concern for its top people)

Long-term disability insurance and salary-continuation plans (useful more for retention than performance improvement)

Individualized retirement plans

While benefits have limited motivational value, they can be useful as compensation tools because of their tax-saving advantages. Smaller companies can exploit the advantages more easily than larger companies, because they can more easily individualize the choice of benefits.

PERQUISITES

"Perks" are the individualized cash and noncash benefits that set individuals, usually executives, apart. They are usually modest in cost but high in motivational value. The costs are kept in check by IRS rules of reasonableness, but the range and quality of perks are sufficient that most executives will put themselves out to earn them.

Following is a list of the more common perks:

Company cars

Club memberships

Officers' and directors' liability insurance (more a necessity than a perk, especially in publicly held companies)

Personal liability insurance (using the company's insurance-buying clout to get desirable coverages and costs)

Company dining room, apartment, plane, or private rail car (requires taste in the light of the company's business)

Financial consulting (for income tax, investment, and estate planning)

Use of corporate buying power to buy personal items at a discount

Chauffeur (an unusual but effective time-saver for those who have to drive a lot. To avoid the embarrassment most managers feel in using a chauffeur, consider using one at least part-time when the time of a manager is being wasted for commuting or routine travel among several locations)

But be careful in individualizing benefits. Unless you emphasize the trade-off aspect (choosing one benefit means giving up another), you are likely to set a precedent for others demanding the benefit. Add to the list of available benefits slowly, because they quickly become chiseled in granite and seen as part of normal pay rather than as extras. After providing the benefits required to hire and keep people, you will probably do better to delay adding benefits until you are confident they are affordable and not likely to be dropped in the future.

One technique to make the best use of your fringe benefit budget is to set a standard of corporate performance to be exceeded before you add more benefits. Then, after the standard has been reached, create a formula to provide the funds for more benefits and permit the employees to decide which benefits they want. Knowing they will continue to receive the new benefits only as long as the company continues to achieve its performance goals, they are likely to be conservative in their choice.

Individualizing compensation is discussed further in the next section.

BONUSES

Base pay is critical to maintaining standard performance and retaining employees, but it is the hope of added income that focuses the mind and energy on attaining extraordinary results. The compensation packages of key executives in companies that really want such results contain rewards for achieving them. The rewards are usually short-term, based on at least reasonably measurable results, and can be the most motivating element in the total compensation package.

The reward system bears heavily on the quality of risk-taking in a company. Most managers try to avoid risks—to conserve their gains, to please their boss, and to serve other interests which do not foster corporate strengthening or growth. Bonuses are used as a device to encourage approved behavior. But smart firms use bonuses differently: to encourage striving for superior results. Where so used, they serve the purpose well. Where they are not so used they serve no useful purpose; they have become part of the salary system. Therefore, they should be keyed to risk and results. Bonuses paid to those who have risked nothing do not motivate and drive out innovation.

Incentive bonuses generally range from 10 to 50 percent of base salary; some are limited to a percentage of base. Others are unlimited, except as the IRS may raise a question of reasonableness, rarely the case with non-shareholders.

LONG-TERM OR CAPITAL ACCUMULATION

Most managers do not accept Social Security as an adequate reward for spending the bulk of their working lives with a company. Therefore, pension and profit-sharing plans, deferred compensation, and other means of capital accumulation are used to reward long-term employees and permit them to build an estate through IRS-approved tax-saving devices. Because key executives in smaller companies are few, it is possible to negotiate individual plans to satisfy individual needs. Deferred compensation contracts, shadow (performance) shares, or stock appreciation rights, and capital stock distribution through sale, gift, or bonus are some of the available techniques.

OTHER FORMS OF PAY

The following list summarizes other forms of pay you might consider.

   Lump-sum payment of a salary increase—the company takes back a note covering the unearned portion of the payment if the employee leaves before the end of the year.

   Participation in off-balance-sheet partnerships that lease assets to the operating company. A competent tax advisor can help set up such a partnership, which permits company rental or lease payments to be made to a partnership of family members or other dependents of managers who are otherwise ineligible to receive corporate payments.

   Personal items and working conditions (office decor, flexible hours).

   Resort locales for annual planning or board meetings.

   Originally proposed as a means of maintaining workers' commitment to capitalism through their beneficial interest in a company's equity, Employee Stock Ownership Plans (ESOPs) were also touted as a way to raise capital which would be paid off with pre-tax dollars. Although there is some evidence that an ESOP will enhance employees' interest in their work (especially where the company's viability is questionable), in most cases the payoff of increased corporate net worth and the relationship between an individual's contribution and improved profits are too remote. Furthermore, the beneficial stock interest of each participant is subject to the non-discriminatory ERISA rules, which prevent targeting extra stock to key personnel. Because an ESOP is useful largely in special situations, smaller companies should get the best counsel available before adopting one.

Participation in equity growth—stock; performance (shadow) stock plans are a means of computing how an individual can participate in a company's growth without making an investment or changing the ownership percentages.

Individualizing Compensation

The benefits of individualizing compensation, tailoring it to personal needs, are evident. Smaller companies are the principal beneficiaries; they can more easily fit their pay plans to individual needs than can larger ones. They are not limited by salary grade systems or other restrictions. Setting individual pay has some problems, but they are usually fewer and less serious than those resulting from trying to compress different needs and jobs into a bureaucratic straitjacket.

By setting a percentage of base pay or a flat amount for each manager or employee in a cafeteria plan, you permit each person to choose from a list of those benefits *he* wants. Although a cafeteria plan adds some adminstrative problems, it is feasible and shows employees you care about them as individuals.

Individualized fringes are targeted to individuals and therefore must be treated with wisdom as well as discretion. They invite invidious comparison and the curiosity of the tax collectors. You have to lay down clear rules of why they are given, analyze cold-bloodedly the effect of the rules on management style and tone, and decide on the shade of grayness of their tax consequences.

If you want to use pay to direct behavior by setting it for each manager, you will have to hold individuals accountable for results and measure how much of the results they achieve. The achieving manager will work harder and more creatively if she knows that her pay is realistically connected to what she alone produces.

The concept of accountability is not limited to managers. Studies of janitors and maintenance personnel show that they respond to accountability. When they and their supervisors can clearly identify each individual's areas of responsibility and rewards and punishments are tied to satisfying individual goals, performance improves.

Avoid situations in which one manager can earn more only at the expense of another. A win-lose plan is destructive to teamwork. If you cannot separate individual accountability and results, use group pay.

Another way to individualize compensation is through the bonus system. Design the system so that employees can earn more on the basis of their individual contributions. That serves two useful purposes. It provides a basis for self-motivation and a method for social recognition, both effective behavior determinants.

In our opinion, incentive bonuses should be without limit. But they should be based on the realities of the individual business. That means they should never be paid out of the funds needed to keep the firm alive *except* when such bonuses are the means for keeping the company alive.

Two basic decisions must be made when setting up bonus plans: how much is to be put into the bonus fund (which includes the basis for computing the bonus) and how is it to be divided? The answers depend on the results sought. Therefore, they should support company objectives. Without such objectives, performance appraisals and bonuses cannot direct managers in the right way.

Bonus planning should include the following considerations:

1. The plan should create competitive advantages. That requires that the firm's competitive advantages be understood by everyone as an actionable goal.

2. It should reward people for creating those advantages.

3. The plan should deal only with critical issues. The point is based on the psychological principle that people can concentrate on no more than five or six objectives at a time.

4. Everyone who contributes to the results should participate in the plan.

Incentives should be designed to produce better results, not more effort. One is not a function of the other. Getting managers to put in more time will usually produce few benefits for a company. Ten hours more a week from managers will not solve more problems or solve them faster. It will probably add to the list of problems. A manager who regularly works more than forty-eight hours a week is probably incompetent and a threat to his company, not an asset.

The best way to get managers to be more effective is to get them to change their priorities, to use their time differently. Everyone optimizes, that is, behaves so as to achieve the best trade-offs between effort and rewards, as perceived by the individual. Since employees control their efforts, but you control the rewards, the best strategy in raising productivity is to tilt the trade-offs in the direction of maximizing by raising the rewards that can be earned for the results you want.

Everyone, key people included, lopes along at less than capacity—around 50 or 60 percent—most of the time. If you want employees to sprint more often and increase their "speed" generally, offer exceptional rewards that they can capture *at their will.*

Special Problems of Smaller Companies

Compensation is seldom a productive force in smaller companies. Most of them think of compensation as an unpleasant necessity, something that has to be given for services rendered, rather than as a resource that can be used to produce desired results. The connections between compensation and personal pride, commitment, initiative, and productivity escape most small company managers. They tend to deal with these connections without objective knowledge of the nature of compensation. Since compensation will have a great influence on corporate effectiveness, managers of smaller firms should know what it can and cannot do.

Like any other resource, such as working capital or production materials, compensation offers all firms many opportunities to realize their aims more efficiently. Since smaller companies cannot operate as do larger companies, their managers should search for ways to use compensation that exploit their size advantages and offset their size disadvantages.

A difficulty in compensation planning in smaller companies is organizational. These companies are too small to afford a full-time manager of compensation. As a result, compensation planning tends to be episodic and performed by nonspecialists. Smaller firms usually pay attention to compensation only when forced to by the prospect of losing key people or by the need to secure additional staff to cope with rapid growth. Even then, systematic compensation planning takes second place to adjusting compensation as the need arises and satisfying short-term growth problems on a patchwork basis.

Another problem smaller firms have is their susceptibility to the prejudices and false assumptions of their top managers. It is far more difficult in larger firms for compensation to be dominated by the subjective views of an individual or group. Smaller firms, often owned by individuals and families or run by single-minded executive groups, do not have that protection.

An example is the effect that struggling through the depression had on the manager of a small company. Money had been so critical to his family's survival that he was convinced that only money would motivate people. Even in the best of times, when money had lost its primacy among signs of success, he refused to use other rewards or to try other motivational techniques. His managers grew old around him caring for what the creative people, no longer with him, had left behind.

Advantages of Smaller Companies

Being smaller does not keep firms from being effective in their compensation planning. It just means they have to use different means to attain the same ends, equitable and behavior-controlling pay. Probably the biggest advantage smaller companies have in compensation stems from the smaller size of their key decision-making groups. Studies show that companies of all sizes are disproportionately influenced by the efforts of a limited number of people. As few as a half-dozen executives can set the strategy and working climate of giant organizations. The advantage to smaller companies is that the number of such executives is so low that the chances of misunderstandings and counterproductive decision-making and actions are also low. The key people should receive special consideration in compensation planning. Smaller firms are in a much better position to implement that principle than are larger ones.

Managers, like companies, come in different shapes and sizes. There are the builders or initiators, the maintainers or custodians, and the harvesters or liquidators. Each has value, but managerial tigers cannot be paid and held on the same basis as maintainers, those who support growth but do not initiate or produce it, or liquidators, those who are best suited to putting an end to what others have started. Pay all three types the same, and the tigers will leave.

Tigers constitute approximately 10 percent of the managerial population. They gravitate to jobs and companies where they can set reasonable goals, enjoy the freedom to implement them, and control their activities through useful feedback. An essential element of feedback is the pay for reaching the preset goals. The more substantial the pay, the more effective the feedback.

Maintainers and liquidators need fair salaries, fringes, and some participation in profits to keep them effective. But they are not as rare as tigers and they are more easily replaced. But key movers are not, certainly not within the time frames required for their replacements to learn the business and how the organization functions and to become leaders. One way to retain tigers is to see that they do not need to invest time in being concerned about their compensation.

In most cases that is not too difficult to do. The amount of current cash required to keep the involvement of key people high is small in proportion to total cash needs. It is cheap money when courageously but carefully spent.

The compensation policy for tigers in smaller, growing companies should be base salaries at the low end of a competitive scale, followed by a substantial participation in the pretax income earned over a high ROI. The ROI to be earned before the bonus is computed must be high enough to satisfy the company's growth and other financial needs, such as equipment replacement. An arrangement that pays a bonus on the earnings over the ROI goal costs nothing for average performance and little when the high standards are exceeded. Incentive bonuses between 40 and 100 percent of low base salaries can be dramatically motivating. And they are affordable, since the bonuses can be designed to be paid only from incremental profits.

Another advantage of smaller companies is that compensation need not be as sensitive to conventions and common influences as it is in larger firms. For example, to keep from disrupting local economies the bigger companies have to be very careful in setting pay scales in communities with no other employer their size. Smaller firms, because they are less responsive to convention and trends, need not follow large-company pay policies; however, they must be careful not to fall victim to the prejudices and false assumptions of their top managers.

Compensation Practices that Demotivate

As you work on a compensation program, it may be helpful to have a list of things to avoid.

GIVING EQUAL RAISES TO ALL

Giving equal raises to all usually stems from the desire to avoid face-to-face individual appraisals. The policy produces short-term superficial peace but more ill effects than good. Giving equal raises in absolute amounts or in the same percentage relationship to base pay only turns off the few outstanding performers.

GIVING SMALL RAISES

If you want your good people to look for jobs elsewhere, give small raises when you can afford to give more. These days, most employees expect a 6 to 8 percent raise for adequate or better performance. But that is not enough to support a significant rise in living standards or justify a major change in effort. To keep star performers you may have to give them annual raises of 15 or 20 percent or more.

PAYING TOO MUCH MONEY TO TOO MANY PEOPLE

When a compensation program provides people with more money than they deserve, it reduces their initiative and quality of risk-taking.

When more money is paid than is deserved and required, either there are too many good people for the work to be done, or, more likely, ordinary performers are being rewarded at the same rate as good ones.

MAKING DIFFERENCES IN PAY LEVELS INSIGNIFICANT

A clever way to shut off the flow of creativity and exceptional effort is to reward outstanding contribution with a niggardly reward. It comes as a jolt to anyone, accustomed to small rewards or not, to receive a bonus close to those received by ordinary producers.

KEEPING OUTDATED PAY DIFFERENTIALS

Another way to stifle creativity and exceptional effort is to maintain differences in pay long after the circumstances that justified them have vanished. For example, three brothers joined the family business when they emerged from college or army service. Their father set their pay as they entered the firm. Twenty years later (ten years after their father had died) the three brothers were still keeping the same pay differentials. We could find no relationship between what they were earning and what they were worth. However, their dissatisfaction with their pay was proportionate to their contribution.

PUTTING A LIMIT ON BONUS PAY

An effective way to demotivate people is to put a limit on their bonus. Limits are usually interpreted to mean either that management cannot measure performance, or, if it can, does not understand the importance of high performance. Either way, the firm loses. It loses the interest of employees in operating at the outer edges of their competence, or it loses employees' confidence in the firm's management.

PUTTING THE COMPANY LAST

As dangerous as ignoring issues of pay is putting pay before company health. Since the health is the woof upon which the warp of individual pay is woven, no good employee wants to benefit at the expense of his company's financial health.

Case in point: Because the sales group of a printing manufacturer included a large number of shareholders, the sales representatives had the right to negotiate the price of sales made, on which they were paid a 5 percent commission. One result was that they managed to get rich by cutting prices while the company floundered. When the system was changed to pay commissions on the gross margin of each sale, no sales representatives quit. They simply worked harder to keep up their income. Sales volume and profits both rose.

CONFUSING OWNERSHIP AND COMPENSATION

Did you ever work in a company where one fork-lift driver made the equivalent of $50,000 a year because he was a son of the owner? As consultants we did, and have seen similar situations elsewhere. Aside from the situation's standing as a running joke, it was also a constant irritation to others, particularly those inclined to working hard to do well for themselves and the company.

If you want to keep good people working for you, keep incompetent uncles, aunts, and nephews off the payroll. Do not put the family first. The basis of that advice is that if the company's assets are not respected by its owners and the owners are not rewarded on the basis of contributions to the firm, employees cannot be expected to respect the company's assets or their use of time.

SAYING ONE THING, PAYING FOR ANOTHER

Because pay is the clearest signal of the results you want, make sure that what you pay for and what you say you want are consistent. You effectively alienate the people who do what you say you want when you pay for something else. A typical example was the wholesaler who advertised and talked to his staff about service, but gave out promotions and raises largely to those who brought in new customers.

USING LONGEVITY AS THE SOLE BASIS FOR PROMOTION

Promoting on the basis of length of employment is guaranteed to accomplish two things: it will create incompetence where none existed before, and it will deprive you of the competence available to you No employee with potential or capabilities already proved will work hard for an incompetent manager or will wait long until the incom· petent manager leaves the job. The icing on the cake of the competent subordinate's discontent is the pay differential which, tradition demands, favors the boss.

BEING INSENSITIVE TO COMPENSATION ISSUES

Never treat a question about compensation lightly. Doing so tampers with the healthiest element in the effective employee, her self-respect.

Our rule of thumb is that the most pressing issues in regard to pay are raised by the most valuable employees, the ones most confident about their skills. You cannot ignore them without penalty. Also, remember that what to you may seem trivial amounts or problems are not to others, who often have to overcome fear in raising the issue at all.

FIRING PEOPLE INSTEAD OF CUTTING THEIR PAY

The Peter Principle states that a person eventually is promoted to the level of his incompetence, from which he cannot be promoted any further. Another side of the Peter Principle suggests that the incompetence existed before the person was promoted and either was not recognized or was ignored. Either way, the person's incompetence is not the only one involved.

Mistakes made in promoting people beyond their competence usually end in one of two ways: firing the person or keeping her on while reducing the demands of the job. Neither is an optimal solution, and the second can be deadly. A better alternative in smaller companies is to give the person who has failed an opportunity to return to her old position or another one suited to her skills and take a pay cut appropriate to the new position.

More on this subject will be found later in this chapter.

The Starting Place in Compensation Planning

Effective compensation planning begins with setting high-quality company goals and objectives. When a compensation plan is directed toward reaching corporate goals and supports the firm's strategies, it becomes itself a clearly defined strategy of accomplishment. When there are no clear or communicated corporate purposes, much time is spent answering questions about priorities in decision-making, action, and where time should be spent.

Compensation planning cannot tell you what business to be in, what to sell or to whom, what organizational structure you should have, nor how to resolve departmental or personal conflicts. But it can create a sense of consistency and purpose by giving prominence to the key results the company wants and the type of behavior it will reward. First-rate, well fitting goals and objectives must exist first. Where they do not, save your money. Just pay what you have to, which in most cases is what your employees can realistically get elsewhere. In this case, you do not need to *plan* compensation.

In your efforts to develop motivating goals and objectives, keep in mind the inverse proportion rule: the further away the results horizon, the less the motivational value of the goals and objectives. Because they are usually so results-oriented, key managers frequently are reluctant to commit themselves to projects with payoffs several years away. Compensation is an important element in solving business problems, but it is rarely *the* answer. While many business problems cannot be solved without considering pay, it is also true that dealing with pay alone will rarely cure a business problem.

Compensation problems almost always have their roots elsewhere. If the deficiencies other than those of pay are not corrected, compensation planning will go awry again.

Here are a few guidelines about how people feel about their work and their companies:

1. Most people want to respect the company they work for and the person under whom they work.

2. People want job security. Where reasonable job security is not provided, compensation has little power. Most people, including tigers, want job security to the extent that they feel they control whether or not they shall remain employees. Where they feel that control is in others' hands, they are not free to contribute individually and fully; they are too busy worrying about whether they will have a job next month or looking for a job in a firm where they will not have to worry about that subject. When employees are insecure, they do not have much time to be concerned with the equity of their pay or how they can earn more.

3. People want respect from their boss. Most people need the support of others' opinions to develop feelings about themselves. (Martin Buber, the German-Jewish philosopher, said that one of the ultimate goals of being human was to reaffirm the humanity of others.)

4. People want to be respected for their work. They define themselves by the value society places upon it, and by what they are paid for it. Therefore, all work should be made decent. True, some jobs need to be dignified more than others do. These are the jobs which do not produce visible results or do not directly affect profits, do not demand high levels of skills, or are dull because they offer little stimulation or variety. But all work essential to an accomplishment is *essential*, and it should be valued accordingly. If people would not dig ditches, ditch diggers would be more appreciated than would architects.

It may help a manager trying to decide how to measure his people, set up a pay system, and communicate the plan, to remember that each of these non-monetary needs has a substantial impact on the commitment and motivation his people will apply to the job.

Guidelines to Effective Compensation Planning[1]

Attract the Right Number and Kinds of Managers. A compensation program should attract good people, especially the type of people needed to implement a competitive market strategy. Even when you think you are well and fully staffed, designing your program to provide salaries to attract competent outsiders will be of benefit. It will constitute one more check that you are paying your current employees correctly. If you offer salaries to outsiders equal to what you are willing to pay insiders and you get no takers, you are probably not paying your people enough.

Pay for Performance. Next, the program should be designed to retain the firm's good performers and to make the company unattractive to inadequate performers. The latter point is simpler than it sounds; design the program so that it does *not* attract or retain the people whose skills or risk-taking are inappropriate to the company's needs.

Raise Performance to Outer Limits. Compensation should be used to encourage people to perform at high levels. However, be careful not to fall into the trap of thinking that more money necessarily will raise performance. Money *alone* seldom raises the performance of those who matter. For most people work satisfaction is more related to retention than to compensation, especially when the latter is fair and equitable. Therefore, if pay will not affect performance and profits, there is usually little reason to change pay.

Case in point: a fifteen-store retail chain paid its managers salaries which were low but reasonable in the small towns in which they lived. Concerned about the chain's low overall profitability, the CEO looked into the possibility of raising the pay and bonus of the store managers. Upon analysis, it became clear that the factors that caused profitability, such as location, merchandising policy, pricing, advertising, and inventory levels, were not under the managers' control. Under those conditions, raising store managers' pay would not materially improve store profits.

[1]Adapted from Theodore Cohn and Roy A. Lindberg, *Compensating Key Executives in the Smaller Company* (New York: AMACOM, a division of American Management Associations, 1979).

Pay for Results. The most successful compensation programs pay for results, not activities, and for outputs, not inputs. Therefore, effective compensation policies direct behavior toward achieving the results that will help the firm reach its goals. They give proper weight to individual and group contributions, and differentiate sufficiently between routine and extraordinary performers so that outstanding performers can be rewarded proportionately.

Keep the Firm Competitive. At the least, effective compensation plans maintain a firm's competitive ability by not putting it at a disadvantage in hiring and retaining good people. However, compensation not only attracts and retains employees; it also makes them affordable. Pay levels must be competitive, if only because personnel costs are usually the first or second largest operating cost of all companies.

To make compensation competitive you have to match salaries paid for equivalent positions in your areas, particularly those paid by competitors. Competitors are not just those companies who compete for customers in the marketplace. They include any firm to which an employee might consider applying. For people who have easily transferable skills, such as engineers, computer experts, and accountants, job competition includes just about every company.

You must also be prepared to lose someone whose salary demands rise above the upper limits of reasonableness. Almost all firms, especially those with minimum growth opportunities, will lose managers able to command a greater salary than justified by their performance evaluations and local wage levels. However, if your evaluation and salary level procedures are sound, these situations should be rare.

Be Seen as Fair. A compensation plan cannot be effective if it is not seen as fair. It must give evidence that comparability has been considered and it must be clear about what must be done to earn more.

Most people make judgments about their compensation with inadequate knowledge, because they rarely know what other people do and usually lack information needed to compare their performance with others, especially when they are working in parallel. Managers of stores, departments that do not work with each other, design engineers working on different projects, accountants and lawyers working for different clients—all are working on parallel lines and have inadequate exposure to the work of others. They are ill-equipped to compare their salaries with others. Nevertheless, they do compare. Therefore, an effective compensation plan is written to support comparisons, not suppress them.

In a professional organization, an attempt was made to use the input of the principals on each other's performance to help divide the firm's profits. Two discoveries were made: each person evaluated his own contribution several places higher than others did; and only a few top administrative managers, aware of the contribution of all individuals, could base their evaluations on information, not gossip or past reputations.

A compensation policy seen as unfair will probably demotivate those people who have the highest responsibility, take the biggest risks, and produce the most for the company.

Employees with a well-founded sense of their worth also compare their pay with what they can earn in jobs they think they can fill in other organizations. A well-publicized example is the salary and fringe package bargaining by baseball and basketball players when they use the amounts paid other players as a floor for their demands.

Awareness of what the market will pay does not necessarily show that people are looking to change jobs. It indicates that one of the recognized measures of their worth is their comparative earnings.

Productive employees want their self-evaluation corroborated tangibly. They want to feel they are not being exploited. They want to be able to say: "In this area, in this type of job, I am worth $_____ to $_____, and I'm in that range."

Managers should explore and jointly plan the pay programs with key people to get their reactions and suggestions before resolving the philosophy and details. It is arrogant, and therefore stupid, to impose a compensation program, especially an incentive plan for key managers, from above without first checking its reasonableness with those involved. This suggestion is based on sensitivity to the changes in professionalism and what people expect of their work and their employers: an understanding that pay is too important a symbol of an individual's independence to permit it to be settled unilaterally.

Meet the Varying Needs of Employees. All people do not want the same things out of life. Therefore, it is unrealistic to expect they want the same things out of their compensation. An effective plan takes into account that peoples' needs differ in accordance with their individual situations and perspectives.

Age, family size, education, and health affect amounts and character of employees' income needs. Within the bounds of fairness, sound compensation planning is tailored to individual needs. With computerization, today that is administratively feasible.

Pay Special Attention to the Needs of Key People. The half dozen (rarely more, except in flat organizations such as professional groups) key people who govern the performance of smaller companies are the ones most affected by pay inequities. In keeping with the need to pay all people adequately, a good compensation plan provides the kinds of pay needed to keep key employees key and in the firm.

Performance should be separated at different levels of contribution. If you cannot identify exceptional performance and pay for it, you will alienate the key people. They do not like to be lumped together, in terms of pay or other forms of recognition and reward, with run-of-the-mill producers. If you do not want to provide outstanding pay for outstanding output, then you might as well pay for seniority, charm, looks, height, weight, punctuality, family, or anything except a real evaluation.

Key employees with skills in demand are generally more aware of salary levels outside the company than within. A manager administering a pay system should constantly monitor the salaries and total fringe benefit package of those with whom his key people are likely to be comparing their pay.

People probably get more upset about discrepancies in pay than almost any other personnel matter. They relate pay differences to differences in educational requirements, experience, pressures endured, amount of supervision of others, difficulty of the job, unpleasant work conditions, and so on. Try to match job differences with pay differences.

Small company managers who lose key people to larger competitors find the excuse that the employee left solely for money convenient. Although large companies use financial inducements to reach out for desirable employees, salary differences more often mask basic dissatisfactions with the type of work, opportunity for advancement, and frustration in not being able to become a shareholder or have a say in major decisions. Salary differences as the reason for leaving are usually more acceptable than other reasons, many of which imply managerial inadequacy.

Keep Options Open. A well-designed compensation plan does not lock into design features or become the basis of immutable pay decisions. Well-run companies are willing and quick to change their plans as they learn more about their people, the relationships between pay and performance, and competitive compensation practices. You should not take the risk of letting a competitor outrun you because you were ignorant of his more flexible and imaginative compensation program. Skilled managers tend to be experimental in designing their compensation plans. This is not weakness—it is a sign that pay is too important to be frozen.

The unfreezing of a long-established plan should be started as soon as it is unfair to any party. Two top sales managers benefiting from a commission arrangement which gave them a disproportionate and, from the company's viewpoint, competitively disadvantageous share of the gross margin, were unhappy when the plan was adjusted downward. Asked if they would have objected if the original plan had worked against them, they had to admit that they would have taken the initiative to change it.

Fact Gathering Methods

Principles are necessary tools in constructing any system. But, to be useful, they have to be coupled with specific, factual data. The most practical methods for gathering the data, which in combination with the principles can provide a solid foundation to compensation planning, are job evaluation systems and salary surveys and other compensation surveys.

JOB EVALUATION SYSTEMS AND SALARY SURVEYS

Job evaluation methods are primarily useful in fixing base pay. The methods are as helpful in smaller firms as they are in larger. They have developed in response to the need for practical methods for assuring that jobs that are different are paid equitably. Each company, whatever its size, should periodically (every several years or so) review its pay scheme to ensure there is a minimum of salary injustice. Notice the word *minimum*. There is no method available for eliminating actual or perceived injustice, but it can be kept to a minimum.

CONDUCTING YOUR OWN COMPENSATION SURVEY

Where communication is open and managers feel comfortable expressing their feelings about pay, fringe benefits, and working conditions, the feedback needed to update and fine-tune compensation programs is not much of a problem. But where the atmosphere is closed, feelings are repressed, and you need to know quickly what attitudes employees hold in order to adjust the compensation program, consider conducting a survey.

Because the need for a formal survey almost always arises in closed organizations, the survey must provide anonymity and feedback of results in at least summary form to the participants.

In extreme cases, it may be advisable to use an employee task force instead of a survey. A task force has the obvious advantages of independence and of involving employees other than managers.

PREPARED SALARY SURVEYS

Salary surveys are developed by trade and professional associations or by other groups, who publish the results of salary information from a non-random group of respondents. Use them, by all means, but be cautious in interpreting their findings. For example, job titles do not necessarily describe jobs in your organization. Presidents, sales managers, and controllers do not do the same thing in all companies. Surveys rarely relate pay levels to profitability. You should: you pay primarily for results. Unless you know the profits produced by individual managers in companies of comparable size, industry averages can be misleading. However, surveys can help in providing ranges of reasonableness.

The CEO's Pay and Pay Levels

In almost all companies, pay scales relate to the amount paid the top officer. IRS attacks on unreasonable salaries and the CEO's ability to take funds out of the company in fringe benefits and other tax-deductible ways have caused top salaries to rise more slowly than those below the CEO level in many smaller companies. Where the CEO's salary is comparatively low, salary level compression usually occurs because of the pressures of paying increasing amounts to help the lower organization levels staffed with good younger people.

If your pay levels are tight, consider rewarding the special performer by promotion. The tactic has its problems because it may require the addition of new pay levels (which does not eliminate the problem of compression), and it will permit people producing extraordinary results to jump over some with more years in the company. But it will keep the good performer happy. Furthermore, a person moving to a new level will have a greater range of salary growth because she usually starts at the bottom of the new level.

Another technique is to pay bonuses for special performance. The CEO's salary should usually be the highest in the company because it is the upper benchmark of salaries. But the *total* compensation of an effective CEO might be less than some other officers'. Separate the one-time performance with one-time pay by not building the reward into the base. It is smarter and cheaper to give a bonus, even a large discretionary bonus, for solving a problem or handling a difficult situation successfully, than to add to base salary.

Inflation has distorted the allocation of budgeted payroll dollars. Frequently, the bulk of the available funds set aside for raises is used to increase all salaries by some minimum flat percentage to keep everyone even with inflation. The fallacy of this policy is that inflation masks the normal market influence on changes in salary level caused by supply and demand. With no inflation, every employee would not receive the same minimum percentage raise. For example, if computer analysts, engineers, personnel experts, and secretaries are in short supply, the demand for their services will push up their salary levels, completely independent of inflation.

Whether you use a percentage of present payroll or decide on a specific amount, here is a tough-minded method of distributing payroll dollars budgeted for raises:

> Give fifty percent to match changing market levels of salaries. This will protect you from losing critical people who are aware of the scarcity of and demand for their skills.

> Give forty percent to the employees who are at the top twenty percent of your performance standards. This will make clear that outstanding work is the best way to get a raise.

> Give the ten percent balance to the performers in the next thirty percent.

> Some people will receive raises in both the first and one of the other two categories.

This idea is attractive for three reasons: it separates changes in market level salaries for individual jobs from broad and nonmotivating inflationary raises. Second, by giving raises to outstanding performers, it makes clear that only performance will be rewarded. Finally, since every compensation plan leaves some group unhappy, what better group to be unhappy than the performers in the lowest fifty percent?

The Overpaid Manager

The inadequate but well-paid manager can be a heavy financial and emotional burden to a smaller firm, especially when he occupies a high-level position and has long service. There is no problem with the lazy, the cheats, or the frauds; they can be easily gotten rid of. But solving the problem of people who are loyal and still work hard but who have fallen behind the rest of the people in the company is bound to be stressful to any sensitive manager.

There are four major options available to the CEO faced with such a problem:

> He can ignore it.

He can seek to correct the overpayment by omitting increases until the salary comes in line.

He can ease the overpaid manager out.

He can demote the manager and adjust his salary downward.

The first option is a weak one. Although most problems in business are not worth solving, the overpaid manager is not one of them. Even where the key contributors are amply compensated, the presence of a non-contributor being equally paid is almost certainly disruptive over long periods of time.

Too often, CEOs in smaller companies, including those who are aware of the problem, choose to live with it rather than deal with it. After all, it is hard to shake up a person you see often and who may have stood by you when the going was tough. But ignoring the problem is destructive both to the employee and other employees. It is destructive to the employee because she *knows* she is getting paid more for her contribution than are others; it is destructive to the others because they know they are being paid less for their contribution than she is.

Since people usually know what others in the company earn, whether the salary levels are announced or not, the only ones who get hurt when inadequate people are overpaid are the adequate people. Remember, the absolute amount is not the issue; the relative amount is. The gripe is not that *he* is making $100,000 while I am getting $98,000. The gripe is that I am working my tail off and *he* is getting $2,000 more.

The second option, to correct the overpayment by witholding increases, has its own problems. This option is a billboard that advertises a lack of urgency on management's part. Giving less than the inflation rate in raises, or no raises at all, so that the superior people can gradually pass the laggard has little saving grace. The person being bypassed will feel as if he were naked in a shop window.

The third option, letting the problem manager go, involves great generosity if it is to be done free of feelings of guilt. Generosity in these cases is definable. A good rule of thumb is that when you have made a decision to get rid of an old faithful and want the separation to be kind, expect to give a separation allowance of one month's pay for each year of service.

In one case, a manufacturing company with a sales volume of $4 to 5 million had a fifty-year-old manager the owner felt was overpaid by 50 percent. The man had done nothing wrong; simply, he had given all he had to give. Keeping him on any longer would increasingly handicap the firm. The decision was made to let him go. Because the manager had worked for twenty years he was given twenty months' pay, about $120,000, to be paid on a declining basis over five years. The intent was to bridge the gap between what the man could earn on the outside and what he was currently earning. The cost to the company of being generous was not as exacting as it seems. On a present value basis, it cost about $45,000 after taxes.

Because it is generally a lot easier to get a job when you have one, the manager was also given three months on full salary. He was allowed to buy his company car at book value. His insurance was maintained for a year—or until he replaced it. And the explanation as to why he was leaving—that a younger manager was taken on to provide succession—was agreed to in advance.

The manager was given these benefits because, while fifty is not the end of the economic world, his outside employment opportunities were few.

A variant of the third option is to retire the person early. It is possible, with people old enough, to do that in a fair way.

One company we know is taking this option with a sixty-two-year-old executive. Although he has only been with the company ten years, he is receiving almost twenty months' separation pay rather than the ten months' the rule of thumb would call for, because at sixty-two this man would have a tough time finding a job.

The fourth approach, and in important ways the best of all the options for dealing with the overpaid executive, is to keep her in the firm by finding a job she can handle. Even if technology has passed her by, very often a person who has ten to twenty years' experience can stay and contribute a great deal. For example, she can support other people whose technological competence now exceeds hers.

What makes the approach feasible is that most people know when they are doing an inadequate job. Often, all they need to make a change downward is a means for face saving. What they have to accept, however, is the adjustment in pay and fringes that go with the new job.

Most executives given a chance to move to a job they can handle with lower pay will accept the offer *if* they are allowed to do so with dignity. That generally requires the boss of the manager who is being asked to step down to publicly share in the responsibility for the demotion. The alternative has two benefits: it restores the employee to productive work, and it conserves skills and experience the company can use.

If the gap between the overpaid manager's present salary and his *proper* salary is not great, some CEO-owners do not reduce the salary, but absorb the cost to preserve the manager's self-respect.

Assuring Acceptance

To be effective, a compensation plan must be accepted by those to whom it applies. That is best achieved by involving those subject to it in the shaping process.

It is difficult to get everyone involved, time, obligations, and perceptions being what they are, but a committee can help. A committee of three to seven people (management appointed or elected) to set salary levels (not individual pay) and the results to be used as the basis of performance measures can accomplish the aim efficiently. As it gains experience, a committee can also advise as to the number of salary levels, steps within each salary level, and the way the incentive plan should be revised to reflect changing performance and corporate needs.

Lastly, gaining acceptance of the compensation plan requires that it be written and packaged for the main users. If a manual is prepared, it should be attractive, complete, clear, simple, and easily revised. The manual should be given to every employee. To start, disclose salary levels but not individual pay. Disclosure of individual salaries requires a level of trust and openness rare in most companies.

Whether to treat compensation openly or confidentially is not an easy question. What works in one firm can be destructive in another. When there is secrecy about salary levels, raises, and bonuses, those administering pay do not have to explain their decisions, which can save a lot of time. Secrecy also avoids the need to develop a defensible compensation system, rather than one based on someone's intuition and, perhaps, generosity.

Few companies are ready for total openness, because the level of trust required is rare. A lot of time will have to elapse before the typical company will feel comfortable disclosing what individuals earn. Nonetheless, we recommend that salary *levels* be made public to provide a goal for the ambitious.

If you are considering public disclosure of pay levels and the reasons for giving raises and bonuses, be aware that pay will probably be reduced as a motivator unless people see a real connection between pay and performance. When pay differences cannot be clearly tied to performance differences, to avoid personal problems you will probably have to end up with a policy of giving everyone the same raise or bonus or applying the same percentage to base pay.

8 ❦
Training and Development

After employees have been recruited or promoted, you must help them deepen and add to their competences. In this chapter, we discuss some of the issues involved in training and development and suggest methods we think best for smaller firms.

Training Guidelines

There are three major training needs in every organization. They can be expressed as the need for:

1. job-centered or technical knowledge
2. people-centered or psychological, motivational knowledge
3. environment-centered or cultural knowledge

It is clear that who should learn what and how much of it depends on the job. The cashier in the supermarket has to be trained almost entirely at the first level; the supervisor at levels one and two about equally; top managers primarily at the second and third levels. They usually have had training at the first level in earlier years.

How the knowledge is acquired also differs. Among the choices are on-the-job experience, experience from other positions, information from outsiders, classes, books, and audio-visual devices. Smaller firms usually have an outside source of untapped knowledge in their suppliers and professionals. A medium-sized insurance agency used a tax partner from its accounting firm to explain the tax aspects of insured pension plans to its sales staff. The accounting firm in turn asked the insurance firm to provide an expert in casualty coverages to instruct its staff. Both companies benefited.

An assumption behind training is that people are never fully developed. Old and young dogs can learn new tricks *when they consider it worthwhile*. Thus, all development and learning is self-development. The organization can provide the inducement and the means, but the individual decides how much commitment and interest she will give to learning and how much of what has been presented she will retain. About 90 percent of all material is forgotten within a week of its being learned. Only reinforcement and support will increase retention and use.

Developing an effective training and development program in the smaller company requires skepticism. Training results are rarely questioned. Everyone knows that training is necessary and, therefore, it is anti-motherhood to ask what would happen if training were not given. Comparing the performance of those who received training with those who did not is viewed as embarrassing and, in some situations, even disloyal to employees.

The lack of skepticism is especially acute in respect to formal programs offered by prestigious organizations. Smaller companies considering sending people to outside programs should evaluate the programs in the light of their special needs. Get references from people in smaller companies who have attended. Call the instructor to determine whether the material is appropriate for your needs. Ask whether there are other ways of teaching the same information to the proposed attendee. Larger companies have learned to do that. Personnel from IBM, Xerox, GM, and GE are seldom seen at popularly given courses and seminars any more.

Among the consulting and training sources smaller companies should consider are:

1. A local consultant, who is paid an annual fee to stay in touch with the firm's training needs and resources. A college professor with practical experience is often a good choice.

2. Part-time or night courses at a local university. The advantages of this type of program are that it requires a time commitment in addition to normal work from the person who is to attend

(out of town seminars and courses have an element of avoiding work). Because it stretches over several months, such a course favors integration of academic knowledge and daily experience. One of the authors went to school at night while working and can testify that it was all the more worthwhile because what he learned in the evening could be tested during the day. And, as a bonus, it gave him practical experience in managing time pressures.

3. Self-learning courses. The development of many tape-workbook programs has made it possible to study at one's own pace and place. The cost of the courses is usually less than 20 percent of the total cost of attending a two or three day seminar. And, since she learns actively rather than passively, the student's retention tends to be high. Self-instruction materials need not be restricted to purchased units. A service organization faced the need to train ten to twenty new recruits annually. The task fell to whoever was unfortunate enough not to be busy when the recruits came to work in June each year. The solution was a tape-workbook program that could be self-administered. With professional editing, it was sold to the organization's trade association for member use.

4. If the need is sufficiently broad, bring in an outsider to design a program just for your company. There are many competent professionals in this field. Spend the time to check before you choose.

5. If you know non-competing companies in your industry, consider setting up joint training facilities. For example, several groups of accounting firms who are basically non-competitive have formed loose associations with the purpose of developing a level of professional training and review no one firm can afford. Such associations can be far more effective than three to five day seminars repetitively given throughout the country to attendees from a wide range of industries.

6. "Socrates and me under a tree" is bad English but good training. Little can beat the combination of an experienced old hand and an eager young mind. It is our favorite mode of training where judgment is the important element in decision-making. Pick a mentor to guide the experience and theoretical training of the young person. The college tutorial system is worth emulating. The academic tutor assigns books and articles to fill gaps in the regular courses and reviews special papers the student writes, which test her understanding of the basics of the subject. The business mentor reviews experiences and problems, recom-

mends rotation of jobs and supervisors, and suggests courses and books for background preparation.

How to Set Training Goals

Just as business plans are meaningless without a business goal, so is training a waste unless you know what you want to accomplish. The old view that "a little training can't hurt, a lot has got to do *some* good" is not good enough to justify training when the skill and knowledge requirements for survival have risen so high.

Finding what you want to accomplish through training on an objective basis is seldom a simple matter (although for technical training it often is). For example, to determine whether supervisors require training in human relations makes sense only when you can specify standards of good human relations and measure the behavior of your employees against the standards. In the first place, identifying the standards of good personnel relations is complex, and then, measuring actual performance against the standards is time-consuming and difficult to keep free of bias, conscious or unconscious. A friendly attitude toward workers, encouraging participation, stronger feelings toward the company, and a more positive team spirit all sound good, but they are useless as guides to setting up a training program whose effectiveness can be measured. It is almost impossible to determine that any of the above attitudes really exist or bear upon results. A better set of standards for hourly workers to determine the training you want and whether it was accomplished might be:

1. the percentage of the top 25 percent of the work group who were retained for the year
2. the number of employees promoted to supervisor
3. the number of employee suggestions submitted and implemented
4. the maintenance of non-union status
5. the percentage decline in bad work, labor content of finished goods, late deliveries, and formal grievances

Being specific about training results to see whether the input of cost equals some measurable output points to a key fact: *training deals with behavior, not attitudes.*

The purpose of training is to change behavior through knowledge, rewards, and consistency of environment. If attitudes change at all, they do so as a result of a behavior change, not vice versa. For example, assume a manager acts without confidence, showing signs of inadequacy. We observe the behavior but, not being psychologists, probably do not know the reasons for it. Someone exhorts the person to "pep up, snap out of it, feel positive, take charge, grab hold of things." Nothing happens. A superficial attempt to change an attitude changes nothing. Instead, change the performance-environment situation to provide experiences that may help the individual see himself as successful. The successful experience and the experience of success are likely to change both his behavior and his attitude.

In a children's camp, a ten year old camper showed many signs of inadequacy: thumb-sucking, bed-wetting, shyness, and reluctance to join play groups because he lacked athletic skills. To change the behavior and the related attitudes, the counselors gave the boy confidence by teaching him how to swim, light a fire, hit a baseball, and accept simple responsibility for which he was given public recognition. In three weeks a dramatic behavior change took place.

Mechanics of Learning

How people learn is no longer much of a mystery. The following principles are applicable to all learning situations.

1. *Distribution of practice.* Is it better to have an intensive twenty-four-hour weekend cram program or to spread the learning over twelve two-hour periods? Most observers believe that the longer period will result in better learning.

2. *Whole or partial learning.* Which is better depends on both the learner and the nature of the subject. If the subject is complicated and sequential, partial learning seems best. On the other hand, if the subject is simple and short enough to be understood and practiced in one period, the whole learning approach may be better. Where practice is required, learning by parts helps build a stronger base.

3. *Reinforcement.* Psychologist B. F. Skinner's work has been accepted by almost all teachers: its basic tenet is to reinforce positively the behavior you want. Reinforcement can be through immediate recognition, thanks, rewards, acknowledgment of growth and success, or any other way of showing that the learner has done what you want. The application of reinforcement goes beyond learning; it is one of the strongest parts of any good compensation system.

4. *Feedback.* Fast, accurate feedback is essential to learning. Imag-

ine the results of a teacher asking a student in September how much is 2 and 2, the student answering "5," and the teacher correcting the answer in June! The feedback principle is one of the strongest arguments against the sink or swim concept. A person thrown into an experience over her head finds that out, too late, after she has sunk. She will waste a lot of time finding out how to swim, and, in the process, if she survives, may learn the wrong lessons. A better environment for learning is that of the cultivated garden. Choose the right seeds (a radish comes up a big, small, tough, or tasty radish, not a carrot), provide the right environment, and then correct any tendencies to grow improperly.

5. *Motivation*. People learn when they want to, assuming they have the capacity, and will do so when they feel it is worth their while. You cannot do much about capacity, but you can do something about what employees consider worth learning. Therefore, state the potential benefits to learners in concrete terms—possible promotion, pay increase, merit pay, time off, and the like.

6. *Transfer of learning*. The best learning takes place when a practical relationship between what can be learned and what can be applied is clearly established. This principle explains the frustration many people experience and the diminished respect for the firm some people have when they return from a highly touted seminar and find that they cannot apply what they have learned. Because applicability is so readily established in on-the-job training, the learning taking place there has the highest transfer payoff.

7. *Practice*. Behavior has to be repeated in order to be learned and locked in. A consistent, supportive environment increases repetition and improves the possibility that the desired new behavior will be retained. Use all the available techniques to teach people: lectures, conferences, case studies, role playing, games, simulation, laboratory experiences (T-groups and sensitivity training have dropped from their early high place but may still be useful), programmed instruction, and the widest range of audio-visual aids. Merely listing these techniques suggests the need for expertise. A training consultant can make sure that the smaller company uses its limited training resources, especially the time of those being trained, in the most efficient way.[1]

[1] These seven points are adapted from *Training and Development*, edited by Dale Yoder and Herbert G. Heneman, Washington, D.C.: The Bureau of National Affairs, Inc. 1977, pp. 5, 22–23.

The Lessons of Sales Training

To further our understanding of training, let us look at the training of salespersons. Everyone knows you have to train salespersons—but for what? Following are four totally different types of sales training serving four different purposes. (Incidentally, each type of sales activity probably requires a different kind of salesperson.)

1. *Introduce products.* A southeastern distributor was the first in his area to take on a line of Japanese heavy equipment. Although the firm had been in existence for over fifty years and was experienced in distributing American-manufactured equipment, it had never had to face the objections potential buyers raised when asked to consider the Japanese line. Salespersons had to be taught new selling techniques, using role playing to learn how to overcome new objections.

2. *Compete against a market leader.* A lessor of computer equipment realized it could not compete with IBM directly. Its sales program required finding salespersons who were willing to present a balanced view of IBM and be persuasive enough to convince prospective lessees to consider the relatively unknown upstart. The presentation was sophisticated, based on exploiting imaginative financial terms, and required more training in finance than in computer language.

3. *Solve customers' problems.* A specialty chemical manufacturer looks for salespeople with the personal-social skills needed to identify the decision-makers in prospective customers' plants. After a few days of product and factory orientation, sales training consists of studying typical organizational charts, becoming familiar with the general locations of decision centers, and memorizing a list of questions which have been found productive in arousing a prospect's interest. The chemical salesperson does *not* solve the problems. His only job is to find out what they are. A crew of bright technicians back at the factory creates or adjusts the formulas. If the salesperson has the right mixture of nerve, aggressiveness, sensitivity, and greed, the training takes one week. Successful salespersons have been hired who knew nothing about the chemical industry but who had a history of achievement. The training program had one purpose and has accomplished it superbly: fifteen successful salespeople are the proof.

4. *Piggyback selling.* The manufacturer of a well-known women's sanitary product paid a commission of only 2 percent of

sales to an independent sales organization with twenty-eight
sales representatives whose only function was to take the orders
for the product placed by the drug, department, and variety
stores they serviced. Advertising, not the sales representatives,
sold the products. However, in taking orders for the sanitary
product the sales representatives were able to offer related
products. Sales training was simple. For the sanitary product it
required being literate; for the other products it required traditional distributor selling skills.

To summarize, in forming training policies and programs, decide
first what you want as an end result. What specific behavior will
represent a positive payoff from the training effort and cost? What
performance standards do you want your people to achieve? What
is the gap between the current and desired performance? Decide
where in the organization the training should take place. Decide on
the ingredients: the method of teaching, feedback, rewards, and reinforcement. Then evaluate the results.

Qualifying Training as the Solution

Training is often the first solution to which managers turn when they
face any performance problem. The best, and by far the most en-
tertaining, treatment of this issue is *Analyzing Performance Problems* by
Robert F. Mager and Peter Pipe.[2] The subtitle describes the style
"You Really Oughta Wanna."
   Since so much training is wasted because it is not first proven as
a solution to a problem, it is worth mentioning a few of the questions
Mager and Pipe suggest a manager ask about performance deviation
before she invests in a training program. After determining that the
deviation is significant enough to require attention, you should ask
whether the person could perform as desired if his life depended on
it. If the answer is yes—he did it before or it is close enough to
something he did that he should be able to handle it—you then have
to ask why he didn't do it and why he doesn't do it now. If the reason
is lack of knowledge or lack of practice, provide the information and/
or opportunity to practice with feedback.
   If the person can do the job and lack of practice is not the answer,
then ask what the consequences in the mind of the employee of doing
and not doing the task are. For example, is it socially undesirable to
produce up to a management-set standard and, in the process, break

[2]Belmont, Calif.: Fearon Publishers, 1970.

a group-set standard? Since no one follows up, is it worth producing up to standard? Is it punishing to do what is asked (for example, showing up on time for a meeting when it starts only after everyone arrives, fifteen minutes later)? If there are obstacles to an individual's doing a good job, remove them. Close the gaps between organizational and sub-group goals or standards, always measure performance when you set standards, start meetings on time, and include in the minutes who was late. Buried in the foregoing comments is a principle of great importance to those who want to train effectively and raise productivity; namely, that refusal to learn or to perform as wanted is as powerful as it is because it has its rewards. Deviant behavior goes against the norm not because of whim or accident but because it brings some form of benefit afterward. The way to alter the behavior is to remove or counter the benefit. Therefore, make the reward for exceeding the standard greater than for not meeting it.

Mager and Pipe suggest that only after you have examined all *non*-training alternatives to deficient performance should you consider whether training can solve the problem.

Executive Development

Basic training principles apply to executive development, but that topic deserves a few additional comments.

Traditional elements of training include the person, the job, and the environment. Executive development is probably more dependent on the climate in each company than on any other element. Whether a potential manager will have the opportunity to develop his skills depends primarily on his immediate boss's willingness to delegate, share information and decision-making, permit mistakes, and encourage challenge and individuality. It is not by chance that certain people have become famous in business history for their ability to develop others. Alfred Sloan's major contribution to General Motors was less the concept of centralized financial planning and decentralized marketing and operations and more his ability to pick first-rate men and retain them through an exciting, demanding, and rewarding managerial climate.

The difficulty many smaller firms have in developing managers is in respect to the freedom to grow. Entrepreneurs find it hard to let go, to permit others to take over the care of what they have built. No one else can do the job as well as they. In one case, a seventy-five-year-old man appeared finally convinced that he was not immortal and that he needed a successor who should learn the business from the master. The successor came from a related industry and had worked in a large company. He could be described as a professional manager. He lasted three months, the time it took him to realize that the old man was never going to pass the managerial baton.

MBAs right out of school do not do well in smaller companies because their high management potential and training are insufficient to ensure their contribution. When MBAs fail to live up to their potential, it is because they have not realized the need to develop individual styles to match the specific climate of the company in which they are working. The education of MBAs is usually adequate as general preparation for their work to come, but broad, technical training does not always assure, and sometimes hinders, a happy, constructive life in the smaller company. Highly educated employees need training too!

Now, as to the training of a successor; should you designate a crown prince and concentrate your management development efforts on him, or is it wiser to leave the choice of successor open? Picking a crown prince is cheaper and lets you focus your efforts. Leaving the field open reduces the chance of making an early mistake, but is likely to lose the top candidate who is not given the commitment he wants.

Our feeling is that you need to do both, as indicated by the fact that the success ratio in choosing people for management succession far in advance is notoriously poor. If you have identified a few good people, let them know that you are willing to give them a chance, plan for the future, and expose them to the experiences and job rotation which will prepare them for significant jobs. Ask them to make a commitment to stay with you and defer immediate short-term benefits. First-rate people cannot be retained on any basis other than the prospect of exercising power. All other golden handcuffs apply only to second-rate managers or those with limited options. Attempting to hold good people solely by offering salaries and bonuses higher than the industry has two limitations: it can become prohibitively expensive and someone can meet or exceed your pay package. For a smaller company to plan its executive development by using the judicious granting of power as its major carrot is so unusual that it can be a competitive advantage.

9 *⚘*
Coping with Unionism

The organizing of employees has always been seen as a threat by managers of smaller firms. Managers in larger firms accept being organized more as a matter of course. In the sense that unions increase the complexity of running an enterprise, unionization is a threat, and to be avoided when possible. Unfortunately, by the time a firm is faced with an election, unionization is usually impossible to avoid.

In this chapter we offer suggestions to get employees to join with the firm rather than against it.

Why Workers Join

Only a small percentage of employees join unions for positive reasons. Most join because they feel alienated from management; because they feel powerless, unheard, and uncared for as individuals. They react against their facelessness by joining a union, expecting it to bring within reach the power they never felt they had earned on their own.

Management fears unionization for the wrong reasons; for loss of control over production, being stuck with chronic nonproducers, suffering crippling rises in costs, and so forth. The fear is without foundation. Unionization does not further penalize a firm with unhappy workers; their alienation already is penalizing the company. A company that has not been concerned about its workers' states of mind up to the point of its becoming unionized is not much worse off when it becomes unionized than it was before.

Workers' unhappiness at work is a problem that can be as damaging to a company's profits as any single event such as an economic downturn or major accident. It is often the cause of poor attendance, excessive drinking, irritability, poor work performance, injuries, damage to property, and increased turnover, all of which have long as well as short term negative effects.

Many surveys of white collar workers show the most common sources of unhappiness, ranked in order of importance, to be:

1. lack of promotions or raises
2. low pay
3. monotonous, repetitive work
4. exclusion from decision-making
5. problems of supervision
6. heavy work load and excessive overtime
7. unsupportive boss
8. unclear job definitions
9. production quotas
10. inability or reluctance to express frustration or anger
11. inadequate breaks
12. sexual harassment

These sources of stress exist for all hourly workers, whether white or blue collar. And each can be a source of problems, and of the decision to organize.

Summarizing our own experience, we find the following factors drive employees toward organizing:

1. the loss of hope that they will be allowed to participate in decisions affecting their working lives
2. the perception that management has no interest in helping them achieve improvements in pay, benefits, working conditions, hours, or job security
3. lack of faith in the capabilities of top management

4. protection against what is seen to be arbitrary, unreasonable discipline
5. deficient self-image (seeking protection against one's own felt inadequacies)
6. the desire to be with members of one's own race, nationality, religion, social, or other group
7. a pro-union family background

The first four factors can be used as the basis of action to forestall organizing, discussed later in this chapter. The remaining few—deficient self-image, collectivist mentality, and pro-union family background—cannot be so used. However, without the support of the other factors, the last three cannot muster enough votes to unionize a firm.

The First Steps to Remaining Unorganized

Most managers in smaller companies are taken by surprise when confronted for the first time by the possibility of workers organizing. If you have not faced being unionized before and wish not to face it in the future, you can take two steps:

1. Know your workers' attitudes and respond to them appropriately.
2. Keep abreast of efforts to unionize firms in your geographic area and, particularly, in your industry.

The first step in keeping out unions is to know how your employees feel about the company and their jobs. Employee attitudes and how they are likely to affect the company should be researched periodically through formal surveys. The surveys are best conducted by outside specialists skilled in interpreting as well as collecting the information. No company can understand itself fully, and a survey conducted by an outsider has a better chance of being objective than one conducted by insiders. But, if you do not have the time to interview and check on an outsider, don't hold back; do the survey yourself (taking whatever precautions you can against the results being influenced). (*See* chapter 7.)

Our rule is: Never ignore negative attitudes. That action is like trying to outrun an explosion; it can't be done. If you wish to keep unions at a distance, respond to workers' attitudes in terms they can understand and appreciate—and quickly!

The second step is to make it a point to know who is being organized in your geographic area and industry, especially in your size group, and by whom. Do not depend on keeping abreast by tracking only the activities of obvious groups or groups already in existence. New unions or unions you never dreamed would be interested in your company or industry may show up claiming bargaining rights.

For example, a new national union of office workers called, appropriately enough, District 925 has sprung up. It is supported by 9 to 5, a national organization of office workers, and by the Service Employees International Union (SEIU), the AFL-CIO, and the Canadian Labor Congress. District 925 began a campaign to organize office workers early in 1981, installing a toll-free phone line that secretaries and clerical workers can use to get confidential information and assistance in getting organized.

In these darkening days for unions, District 925 may not get off the ground. But then again, the rising number of women in the work force, combined with the persistence of sexually linked compensation discrimination, may make the union venture a success.

Persistence in knowing what is occurring in your area and in the minds of your employees in respect to organizing is essential if you are not to be surprised one day by a letter from a union claiming the right to represent your workers. You can be sure that your company—if it employs a hundred or more line and clerical workers—is never out of the sight of organizers.

Union organizers are sensitive to the inherent or natural reluctance of potential members to be organized. They are trained to be patient, to avoid confrontations or arguments which may alienate, but to be persistant in pushing the union's position.

Keeping Employees on the Side of the Firm

Unionizing efforts have practically no chance of being mounted against firms that treat their employees with the same respect given other resources. (We tend to give the best care to machines and money.) Any company, whatever its size, can try to create a climate of cooperation between employees and management. The history of industrial relations proves that such a climate is a poor one for unions to take root in.

Let us start with the factors cited earlier as disposing employees in favor of organizing. Companies can raise the resistance to unionization by:

inviting employees to participate in making the decisions that will affect their working lives by means of surveys, committees, task forces, suggestion systems, and listening sessions

helping employees achieve improvements in job performance, rewarding improvements in skills with more pay, and offering increased freedom to employ skills to the benefit of the individual *and* the organization

offering incentives to employees to differentiate themselves from their peers by performing better

providing the basis for self-development, for employees being entrepreneurial about enhancing and adding to their skills

identifying promotion possibilities more clearly, and promoting employees as quickly as possible

Taken together, the foregoing responses to the factors favoring unionization amount to recognizing individuality and meeting the needs of employees as individuals.

Smaller firms should take special note of the first and last of the foregoing points, because smaller firms tend to lose sight of them. The first point—that employees want a voice in making some of the decisions that will affect them—rests on the fact that workers no longer accept second-class status. They insist on having a role in determining the environments in which they will work.

The drive to organize in recent years has been far more than a simple reaching for better pay. These days, successful unionization has been due as much to workers' feeling "an impelling need for an organization that would represent their interest in the manipulation of economic power"[1] as to the desire for more pay.

The second point—offering workers opportunities to earn promotions to more interesting and rewarding jobs—rests on the fact that the thrust to organize often arises when "employees, no longer convinced they were Horatio Algers, had to believe or to accept the idea that workers they were and workers they would remain."[2]

"Organization begets organization" goes the saying. We think the principle cuts both ways: the company that wishes to stay unorganized can do so by organizing to be so.

[1]Arnold M. Rose, *Union Solidarity: The Internal Cohesion of a Labor Union*, Minneapolis: University of Minnesota Press, 1952, page 14.
[2]*Why Unions Grow*, by Albert A. Blum, Report Series #98, School of Labor and Industrial Relations, Michigan State University, 1968, page 54.

Diverting Potential Leadership

No groups form democratically; all groups coalesce through the agency of a central idea promoted and sold by a core group or charismatic individual. Workers in a company are not an exception. Until a leader comes along to give movement to their grievances—real or imagined—no organization is possible.

Union organizers are trained to identify the natural leaders in a group. People who speak up, are sought after for advice, or are respected for any reason, are potential union leaders. Because the management of many companies is not as sensitive to the need for natural leaders to find a constructive outlet for their talents, the filling of that need is left to a union organizer by default.

Identifying those capable of exercising influence over their fellow employees is one of the keys to staying unorganized, but only if further action is taken. Employees capable of influencing others should be considered for managerial roles. If persuasive enough to lead employees toward unionization, they probably are also capable of supervising them in work. In any case, such leaders should not be ignored. They should be kept busy enough that their energies are diverted to matters of benefit to the company and to themselves.

Handling Grievances

Most unorganized firms do not have formal grievance procedures, but we are convinced that having one can be instrumental in staving off unionization in firms of any size, as well as in increasing productivity. Progressive, non-union companies have established formal means for resolving grievances that cannot otherwise be resolved quickly and efficiently.

The familiar open-door policy can be effective when implemented wholeheartedly, but it tends to lose effectiveness with time. Grievances eventually take second place to other demands on managers' time, and just a few instances of deferred grievance hearings permanently shut off opportunities to deal with them on management's terms.

Whatever approach is taken to demonstrate that management cares about the way employees are treated, it should be consistent and constant. All efforts to seek redress from real or imagined wrongs should be welcomed, the research surrounding them thorough, and the resulting decisions based on facts and fairness. Fair, in this case, means to the firm *and* the employee. Employees will not be pleased by one-sided victories.

The principal value of a formal grievance procedure is that it speeds up the surfacing and solving of employee problems, thereby keeping them from becoming worse and chronic. In setting up a formal procedure, you need not worry that it will be used frequently. Employees inclined to use the procedure frivolously are few and will be troublesome in any case. You are better off knowing who they are. The bulk of the complaints usually have some merit in fact and should be dealt with quickly and explicitly.

Today, a non-union company should not be without some kind of formal grievance procedure of its own. That is especially true in a social environment which has sensitized workers to the many reasons for which they might feel discriminated against: race, religion, sex, age, or education. Cost-conscious executives prefer to respond to complaints through their own procedures rather than through an uninvited third party such as the government or a union.

Full Employment Practices

One new and growing practice of larger firms worthy of serious consideration by smaller firms desirous of keeping unions out is full, that is, constant employment. Companies that provide security of employment tend to retain their non-union status and management flexibility. Eliminating workers' fears about layoffs (that is, reduction in force independent of performance deficiencies) greatly strengthens employee relations.

Common sense tells us that the policy of full employment is an ideal which ultimately runs against reality. The costs can be significant, but so are the benefits. When times turn bad, companies devoted to full employment have more remedies available to them than do companies that do not practice full employment. When compelled to cut back on labor, full-employment companies can cut back on the work week for all, offer extended vacations or leaves of absence, or employ other strategies that do not diminish their pools of experience and skills. Other companies are forced to rely almost entirely on laying off people in accordance with seniority, which seriously erodes the experience and skills available to them.

Implementing full-employment objectives is not simple. It requires effective coordination between staffing planning and business planning. But the benefits can be significant in the long run. Hewlett-Packard's experience is a good example. By spreading the sacrifice in reduced pay and time among everyone, the company was able to preserve its pool of employee knowledge, experience, and goodwill;

and it had lower indoctrination and training costs when business picked up. The idea is practical for smaller companies.

Involve Supervisors

In your efforts to stay free of unions, do not ignore the possible insulating effects of the supervisory level. Supervisors with whom top management has not shared its worker policies and who have not been trained in human relations can be a barrier to top management's knowing what is going on.

Two mistakes top managers often make are to assume that:

1. supervisors necessarily are on the side of the company
2. having risen to the rank of supervisor, they are good with people

Often neither assumption is valid.

Many of our clients have had benign views of people management which have been valueless because they assumed their supervisors shared and communicated their views when, in fact, they did not. The mistake is common enough, based as it is on the thought that supervisors are part of "management"; they are the loneliest people in most firms and seldom are part of any group, above or below.

It is helpful, where operations justify it, to provide supervisors with a personnel policy manual spelling out how the company wants employees to be treated, how to deal with grievances, how to encourage worker participation in problem-solving, and the like. But do not think a policy manual is the end play in the management-employee game. Personnel manuals do not prevent union elections. Constant attention to workers' concerns does.

How Larger Companies Do It

A recently published study of twenty-six large, non-union corporations suggests nine common attributes, policies, and attitudes that can improve employee relations and productivity.[3] We include abstracts from the report because the factors, in our opinion, are practical for smaller as well as larger firms, and will probably go far to

---

[3]Reprinted by permission of the *Harvard Business Review.* "How Top Nonunion Companies Manage Employees" by Fred K. Foulkes (September/October 1981). Copyright © 1981 by the President and Fellows of Harvard College; all rights reserved.

keep the firms incorporating them in their personnel practices free
of moves to unionize them.

The nine factors are:

A Sense of Caring. Many of the twenty-six companies in the sample
hold strong egalitarian views on how to treat employees. Many of the
usual symbols of corporate rank and status have been eliminated.
Everyone has access to the same parking spaces, receives identical
medical benefits, and eats in the same cafeteria. Executive offices are
lean and undistinguished. Many of the companies permit no perks
such as company cars and club memberships.

Top management's commitment to its employees in these companies goes beyond symbols. For example, Hewlett-Packard is committed to job security, innovative training, internal promotions through
job posting, various profit-sharing plans, and flexible working hours,
all signs that they care about their workers as individuals. These
policies usually came from the top managers early in the companies'
lives.

Carefully Considered Surroundings. The working environment in the
companies is carefully structured to encourage trust and confidence.
New sites for plants are chosen with the idea of how they might help
keep the company non-union. Quality of the local school system,
proximity to a university, and the area's union attitudes are all part
of the consideration in site location. Rural and suburban sites are
preferred, and the number of employees in a single location is limited
to between 200 and 1,200 to keep the relations personal and responsive.

By subcontracting work that unionized employees typically handle,
some of the companies limit exposure to unionization. Working conditions and wages are kept at least equal to those of unionized personnel.

High Profits, Fast Growth, Family Ties. Another important characteristic is close ties between owners and management. Founding
members in some of the companies are still active in management.
In any case, the policies of the founders continue to dominate the
company. For example, IBM's Thomas Watson stated a respect for
the individual which still governs the company.

Employment Security. Many of the companies try to reduce workers' uncertainty about future employment. In its early years, Hewlett-
Packard turned down large government contracts which would have

caused large work load fluctuations. Later, that company cut pay and work time rather than lay off people.

Hiring freezes and using temporary or retired workers are other techniques to keep the work force reasonably stable. Some companies encourage employees to take leaves of absence or to bank their vacation time, both of which permit flexibility in lean times. Another technique is to use subcontractors to handle production peaks.

Promotion from Within. A policy of promoting from within, backed by training, education, career counseling, and job posting, builds employee loyalty. Some companies provide hourly workers with the training and education necessary for them to move into better jobs. Promotion from within not only is a visible sign of concern for people, it builds loyalty and probably increases productivity.

Influential Personnel Departments. Personnel departments in the companies studied are centralized and, therefore, strong. They usually have easy access to top management. In most cases, the Vice-President of Personnel reports directly to the President.

A sign of the strength of the personnel departments is the ratio of one professional personnel person for each one hundred employees. Line managers in many of the companies support a strong personnel department because it helps them keep abreast of workers' attitudes, handle complaints, and conduct performance evaluation.

Competitive Pay and Benefits. The twenty-six companies work hard to ensure that their employees perceive their pay and benefits as equitable. The companies pay well by industry, community, and union-settled competitive standards, but take pains to make sure their employees understand the pay/fringe programs and that their compensation packages are as good as or better than those of unionized competitors. Many of the companies try to eliminate the we/they difference between management and blue and white collar workers by paying factory employees a salary instead of hourly wages.

Managements that Listen. The companies studied use all the techniques available to learn how their employees feel: attitude surveys, sensing sessions, random interviews, meeting with employees from which supervisors are excluded to reduce constraints on getting to true feelings; speak-out programs which encourage employees to ask written questions anonymously; and appointment of an ombudsman, a respected person to whom an employee can go if he feels he has not been treated equitably.

Careful Grooming of Managers. The importance of long-term results, including successful employee relations, is emphasized in the promotion programs of the twenty-six companies. Selection of managers is a key procedure. The training of supervisors who have daily contact with employees receives heavy support. Because concern for the lowest level of worker may have shortcut the role of the supervisor, some companies are paying special attention to the supervisors and are including them in separate attitude surveys. Managers at all levels are spurred to be aware of the importance of good worker relations. Major personnel problems or union-organizing drives are seen as a stigma on their careers.

Dealing with a Drive to Organize

The drive toward organizing a company formally begins with the union's obtaining employees' signatures. That is when the firm's formal campaign to stay unorganized should begin. We say formal only because the campaign is more intense than are the long-term activities aimed at keeping the firm free of unions.

Thirty percent of a company's employees have to sign authorization cards before a bargaining-unit election can be held. The campaign to obtain signatures is usually conducted off company premises and so softly that the company is often unaware that the organizing process has even begun. Therefore, the first problem in coping with a union drive is to detect its beginning. Doing so will give the company a solid lead time in which to counter the drive.

Obviously, the employees behind the organizing drive are not going to announce what they are doing on billboards. Nevertheless, the fact that organizing has started cannot long be hidden, and the firm should be prepared to present swiftly its side in the contest.

The following steps are essential to countering a union drive:

1. Obtain a copy of the signature card and distribute copies with marginal notes which highlight the facts that signing a card can lead to union membership dues, fees, assessments, and support of an organizing strike (the last to stimulate the resistance of those who prefer to be neutral).

2. Inform workers that names of card holders are not necessarily held confidential, and that they have the right to have signed cards returned to them.

3. Use flyers to warn employees that they are likely to be bothered at home, represented by strangers, and lose the right to talk directly to management.

4. Use paycheck envelopes for distributing statements of the company's case; it's legal and effective. Figure 9–1 is an example of one company's statement.

A campaign against unionization has potential pitfalls. Therefore, get expert legal advice before launching an all-out attack. But do not

To All Employees:

As you are no doubt aware, the company has been approached by a union which demands to be recognized as the exclusive representative of the firm's employees.

Whether you want a union to represent you or not is entirely up to you. Here are a few questions the answers to which may help you decide:

— What can a union do for you that you can't do for yourself?

— If a union cannot make good the promises it makes to you, what comeback do you have?

— What individual rights will you give up under a union's constitution and by-laws?

— If you vote a union in, will you be able to vote it out when you no longer want it?

— Do you know what initiation fees, dues, fines, or other charges a union can assess against you?

— Will such dues and other fees that you will be required to pay if you belong to a union be worth the added expense to you?

— Is the union really interested in you as an individual and in your personal development, and how does it propose to help you progress in your career?

— Have you looked into the union's history of financial dealings and reputation for integrity?

These and similar questions should be carefully considered before you finally make up your mind whether or not you want a union to represent you.

Finally, let me assure you that we have no problems that cannot be dealt with if you are willing to do so. We need no third party to help us solve our own problems.

(Signed) President

Figure 9–1. Sample Letter to Employees during Organizing Efforts

fail to counterattack. Sitting back in the expectation that "our people won't join against us" is a sure way to raise the chances that they will.

While planning the counterattack, do not strengthen the union's hand by making last-minute concessions and belatedly trying to win the favor of the organizing leaders among your employees. Doing so is more likely to demonstrate the power of organizing than it is your basic good-heartedness. On the other hand, do not fail to present the outline of a program to meet the more legitimate of the objectives employees seek to attain by joining a union, making clear the advantages of achieving their objectives without the burden of union dues and regulations. Remember, your best argument for staying out of a union is the same for keeping your firm unorganized—the costs outweigh the benefits.

Do not fight needless and employee-alienating battles. Be sure that you are fully acquainted with your firm's obligations in an organizing drive, and that you fulfill those obligations openly. Among the kinds of information that must be furnished to the union according to law are:

Gross wages paid

Rates of pay

Wage and work history of each non-exempt employee

Wage ranges

Wage data concerning another plant of the same employer

Yearly earnings

Overtime and vacation pay of each employee

Average earnings by class of employee

Name and classification of each non-exempt employee

Following is the kind of information usually collected during a union drive:

Number of departments and the operation of each department. The distribution of male and female in each unit. Number of employees in each department.

Job classifications, labor grades, and wage rates. How do these rates compare with organized sections of the industry?

The method of handling complaints and grievances in the shop. What are some of the major complaints within the group? How is seniority observed? Number of workers over 50. Number of workers under 30.

Hours of work and premium pay rates in excess of 8 hours, Saturday, Sunday, and holidays.

Number of paid holidays, vacation schedules, sick leave, and rest periods.

Flagrant violations of state or city health and safety regulations. Lighting, toilets, heating, and special protective laws for women.

Does the company maintain any non-contributory welfare programs? If contributory programs are maintained, check the benefits and costs.

Attitude of foremen and supervisors to employees. Get names of over-bearing foremen or supervisors. Develop list of any arbitrary actions on the part of supervisors which are considered an injustice against any individual worker.

As pointed out above, this information concerning the employees' job is to serve as the major ammunition in the campaign.

10 ❧
Leading Personnel Problems in Smaller Firms and Techniques Used to Solve Them

In preparation for the writing of this book, we wrote to some of our smaller company clients and other smaller companies asking them to name their most important personnel problems and how they coped with them, if they did. This chapter is made up of their answers. We have listed the issues most frequently mentioned and have given a combination of the possible practical solutions suggested by our respondents and our own experience for each.

Issue 1

In the early period of a growing new company or division, people work in a highly informal atmosphere. As the organization grows, it is difficult to develop clear organizational lines and to get the employees from the earlier days to observe some reasonable line of authority without either alienating them or creating a top-heavy and inappropriate bureaucracy.

COMMENT

Size is not a deterrent to clear job responsibilities. One of the most successful managers we have met, a forms distributor, left his original job because, beyond a sales quota, he never knew what a good job was. When he started his own company, he decided his employees would not have the same problem. The first salesperson and the first clerk he hired were asked to write down what they thought the standards of a good job were, to whom they should go for answers to specific questions not covered in a manual, and their questions about job relationships. The standards they provided were used as the basis for performance assessments.

Only in a totally pioneering, explosively growing organization is it difficult to set up clear job standards and relationships. But, even in that case, it is practical and healthy to spend a few hours every six months talking to people about what constitutes a good job.

Issue 2

In the early stages everyone in the company participated, everyone knew what was going on, everyone had access to everyone. Because this was pleasant, we had problems when the town meeting had to be replaced by some combination of a representative or consultative republic or an enlightened monarchy.

COMMENT

Our observation is that the problem does not stem from the changes in the method of passing information around, but from a *decline* in the quality of information passed around. The main reason continued involvement and participation become a problem as a company grows is top management becomes less open, increasingly reluctant to disclose results, plans, problems, reasons for decisions and promotions, and the like. These are signs of a growing insensitivity to the expressed concerns of people.

The obstacle is often based on the false assumption that only owners care about the company. Also, because owners see themselves as having ultimate responsibility for results, they may feel that they dilute their power or have to listen to self-serving drivel if they regularly inform lower level people about activities.

We are sympathetic to the problem, which really has its roots in inexperience. But *our* experience tells us that the period of decline in communications is as costly as it is common *and* unnecessary. There are ways smaller companies growing larger can keep the sharing spirit alive. The most successful company of its kind we know kept that spirit alive through policies established within the business and repeated in every contract and major document written. Another successful company created an in-house management group of non-shareholders, which produced high levels of involvement, company-focused problem-solving, and influence exercised on other employees to think in company rather than in purely selfish terms.

Issue 3

Smaller companies have smaller margins for error. If they permit family relationships to influence job selection and promotion, they are almost sure to make expensive mistakes. Whereas a larger company can often make a key personnel error without suffering disaster, in a smaller company the misplaced relative usually messes up the company. Even if he is not allowed to make important decisions, tolerance of his inadequacy, and his usually disproportionate pay, alienates competent, nonfamily managers.

COMMENT

We think tolerance of family incompetence is far more dangerous than toleration of nonfamily incompetence. Competent producers are not as much affected by loyalty to an employee whose tenure has outlasted his competence as they are by an incompetent protected simply because of membership in an owning family.

Get rid of the problem; you don't need it! Apply the same job and performance standards to family members as you would to anyone else. Do not challenge your father or uncle if he holds voting control, but question the candidacy of a son, daughter, brother, sister, or related spouses, for a job for which he or she has not been trained or had experience.

For example, the president of a family company raised the issue with outside members of the Board of Directors as to whether his younger brother, who wanted the job, was fit to head marketing. Although there was an element of fraternal jealousy in the question, it was truly posed in terms of what was good for the company. The firm had been dominated by a powerful older relative, and was now in the process of developing professional management. After defining the results needed to satisfy reasonable job performance, the outsiders concluded that, although the younger man had no formal training, he had proved in other jobs in and out of the company that he was a fast learner; was imaginative, responsible, accepted by sales representatives and customers as a leader; and, with some training and the help of a once-a-week consultant, was the best candidate available for the job.

A family fight was avoided; the company and the brothers were well served; and the organization got the message that even the president's brother had to pass muster in order to earn a promotion.

Issue 4

"We have had a history of promoting from within. When our business expanded, so did the requirements of our cost system. Growth in the sophistication of results monitoring and cash controls were beyond our controller's ability, and the data-processing installation became the nerve center of the whole company. We had no one who could do the job or was likely to grow into it. For a brief time we had to go outside to fill a key position. How could we have avoided that?"

COMMENT

There is no way to avoid bringing in talent as you grow. The problem is not to keep from going outside, but to keep going outside from causing problems internally. By posing the problem of the controller precisely, the CEO of the above company did not violate his policy to promote from within when he went outside the firm for the technically trained, professional, financial vice-president he needed.

Get the best you can afford from any legitimate source, beginning with the internal staff. You are unlikely to be criticized if you upgrade the company's managerial or technical skills so that everyone can make more money. Furthermore, good people resent personnel decisions which demean excellence or fairness; promoting an incompetent employee or maintaining her in a position beyond her competence will not earn you points for fairness and decency.

There's nothing new about advertising all open jobs to everyone and permitting employees to apply with the same chances as new people. But do so with an *emphasis*; that is uncommon. Often notices of job openings do little more than percolate through the organization. Give them prominence either by making them the subject of special memoranda or putting them in the house newsletter.

Issue 5

"We are not the hottest place in town for young people to start working. Also, since our salaries and fringes only fall in the middle range in the community, we can't use money to attract the new young managers and workers we need."

COMMENT

The firm exploited the CEO's involvement with student athletes in the local high school and university. As an active alumnus and former track star, the CEO encouraged students to work for the company during vacations or part-time during the year. The personal relationships developed made it easier to get candidates to apply for full-time jobs. Perhaps it was a prejudice based on his own experience, but the CEO found that a sports background enhanced work performance. The self-discipline, sense of teamwork, and the superior energy and health of the athlete-employees extended throughout the work force.

The same company also expanded its employment horizons by hiring women for heavy manual jobs that had traditionally been handled only by men, and handicapped people for jobs dealing with the public, again going against common prejudices. Both policies were successful.

Issue 6

"Because of family pressures, young people went directly upon graduation from school into the family business. Should we break this traditional career course and, if so, how?"

COMMENT

Don't let a family member work for the company until she has spent a few years in another business, preferably in a different industry. The experience teaches humility, provides an objective basis for self-confidence and independence, and increases the possibility that the family member will add more to the company than she takes from it in her early years.

Issue 7

"After many years of informal management, we installed a new performance-evaluation system. Soon afterwards we lost some long-time employees. What did we do wrong?"

COMMENT

If your performance standards are fair and tough and you are losing people who are unhappy because they do not measure up in *their* minds or because they feel they cannot move ahead because your promotion policy rewards only competence, don't worry. Under those conditions, turnover is healthy, and you lost the right people.

Issue 8

"We have trouble setting salaries and performance measures for our mid-management group (a $7 million industrial supply distributor). Too much of the decision is based on our feelings about the employees: The 'good old boys' get the raises, while the 'quiet performers' (rarely the same people) get less than they deserve."

COMMENT

There is no substitute for high, clear performance standards. As soon as you let longevity or any other nonperformance factors determine promotion and compensation decisions, you open the decisions to the influence of the flatterer and the self-server.

A leading reason for good people leaving companies is that they feel they have been unfairly treated in promotion or salary decisions. Of course, you will always make mistakes in promoting people or raising salaries, and you won't often satisfy unreasonable or unrealistic expectations. But by doing the job as objectively and fairly as possible, you reduce the risk of losing good managers, of keeping poor managers, and of giving a union a foothold.

Issue 9

"We had a problem that we didn't know we had until our new insurance agent pointed it out. We checked the driving records of all our employees who drove a company vehicle and found that we had a truck driver whose license had been suspended. His nickname with the other employees was 'Crash,' appropriate to his ability to bend fenders. We did ourselves a favor when we fired him."

COMMENT

Good personnel ideas come from everywhere. It costs no more to use the best insurance agent in town than your incompetent brother-in-law, and you will get a lot more for your money. Outsiders can help you in every way, including personnel management. For example, many companies have asked their employees to choose from a shopping list of fringe benefits. A good consultant can suggest alternate packages, which will appeal to people at different stages in their life cycle and at different costs to the company.

Issue 10

"We haven't found a practical way to translate work into size of staff and numbers of people. I have the feeling that we are overstaffed, but have no way of measuring it."

COMMENT

The simplest way to avoid overstaffing is to staff for the slack season. If you are not forced to go to overtime or add part-time help when business is at its busiest, you're overstaffed. Get rid of some people.

By the way, don't sell short the benefits of overtime and part-time workers. Your employees welcome the extra income, and using part-timers helps community relations.

Sources of part-timers abound. They might be off-duty firefighters, police officers, nurses, teachers, recreation leaders—in rural areas, farmers and agricultural workers—and any others who work regular hours and can be scheduled in advance. One company we know uses a live-wire fireman, with the blessing of his chief, as a recruiter for regular part-time help. He is paid a twenty dollar weekly fee for finding and assigning other firefighters to the warehouse, delivery, and counter jobs the company needs filled.

Issue 11

"We want our people to feel that the company's success and their own are the same. If we make money, they should. We struggled with the ways of doing this because it was clear that if employees were to help us to do better, they had to know how we were doing. This meant disclosure of financial information, if only of departmental results, and we were reluctant to share it with employees."

COMMENT

One solution was to set up monthly profit goals and pay employees a bonus over the following four weeks when they achieved the goal. Employees helped set up the goals and were told how they were doing. The concern over disclosures was offset by the need to increase employee participation. The method also offset the problems that arise from paying out bonuses over time.

Spreading out an incentive bonus is often nonmotivating because the bonus becomes an invisible part of the total compensation package. Individual payments lose their relationship to performance. This example is different: the bonus is earned monthly and then paid over the following month. The incentive payments were over a short enough time frame to relate the bonus to the results.

The disclosures necessary to implement this plan led naturally to meetings at which top managers explained to everyone what was happening. In good times it permitted sharing of the good news; in bad times it faced the group with survival issues. Full financial statements were distributed to everyone. Explanations and answers to questions became routine parts of the program. Finally, the company faced directly the common but rarely expressed complaint: "No one tells me what's going on around here." The answer was weekly management meetings with no hidden or secret agendas and immediate dissemination of the minutes to everyone.

Issue 12

"We can't afford to develop our own formal training for our people, yet they must be kept up to date on all the new products."

COMMENT

Training can be offered to everyone. Manufacturers will usually lend sales representatives. Assign the responsibility of explaining new products to the whole staff to different people. Hold the sessions after hours and pay people at the overtime rate for attending.

Issue 13

"We have difficulty in hiring and training people and seem to repeat the same mistake: hiring what seem like competent trainees and then losing them before they start producing."

COMMENT

Finding out why you lose new employees who seemed to have potential requires that you reexamine your selection and introductory employment practices. Start by conducting exit interviews, which should be announced in advance so the employee has a chance to think about the questions. Follow up anyone who leaves three to four weeks later. Call him at home, ask him to come in for a quick talk or, better yet, take him out to lunch.

Because many smaller company managers treat a resignation as a personal affront, the termination is not pleasant and reduces the possibility of keeping communications open. It is helpful to remember that, when they are treated properly, ex-employees and rejected job candidates can be potential salespersons for your company.

The reasons people leave are rarely expressed openly. Showing a nonrevengeful and objective interest is also rare. It may also be the only way of your finding out how to improve your retention rate.

Issue 14

"Top managers seem to be too busy to get the important work done. We'd like to have more useful job descriptions to help them delegate their lower priority work."

COMMENT

Our guess is that 95 percent of all job descriptions are never used. They are a major cause of frustration because they take a great deal of time to prepare accurately and, even well-prepared, they are promptly discarded for real work. *If* job descriptions are to help focus managerial effort, they probably can be written on one page, listing the few key results you want. If you want people to use their time more efficiently, read one of the good books on time management.[1] Most of them require you to write down life, job, and daily goals in priority order, a tall but necessary start.

Delegating is a problem not unique to smaller company managers. But it is harder for them to delegate than it is for managers in larger

[1]Ferner, Jack D. *Successful Time Management*. New York: John Wiley and Sons, 1980.

Lakein, Alan. *How to Get Control of Your Time and Your Life*. New York: New American Library, 1974.

Mackenzie, R. Alec. *New Time Management Methods for You and Your Staff*. Chicago: The Dartnell Corporation, 1972.

Mintzberg, Henry. *The Nature of Managerial Work*. New York: Harper & Row, 1973.

Stokes, Stewart L., Jr. *It's About Time*. Boston: CBI Publishing Company, 1982.

organizations because of the multiple roles played by managers in smaller companies and the high degree of specialization found in larger companies. It is hard to make the jump to telling someone what to do (and letting him do it) from your doing it (faster and better than he can). The way to increase delegation is not through the writing of job descriptions; it is through staff planning, training, and development.

The most persuasive reasons for delegating are to prepare employees to take on increased responsibilities and to assure redundancy of critical skills and knowledge. Personnel development is severely constrained where managers will not delegate.

Issue 15

"We have had to let go people who have been with us for over twenty years. It is tough for everyone. How can we ease the pain and guilt?"

COMMENT

We assume you have explored all other employment alternatives within the company. If no other job is suited to the person, then consider easing the job loss by using career consultants (out-placement specialists) who are available in most mid-size cities. Using them symbolizes the concern of a sensitive smaller company manager for people's lives as well as their jobs. Since few people are surprised at the revelation of their inadequacy and have the resources to act on the awareness, most separated employees appreciate the help a career consultant can offer.

In the company which prompted the question, the terminated employee was helped to face a new life positively. Consider the effect on the rest of the firm of the caring treatment of the old employee.

Issue 16

"We have tried all sorts of compensation for our sales force. Quotas caused conflict; salespersons aimed low, we aimed high, and the result was an unhappy compromise."

COMMENT

One solution was a compensation plan based on the forecast each salesperson made. Two bonuses were made available: one for accuracy of forecasting and one for actual results. If a salesperson aims low and achieves above her forecast, she earns less than she does if she forecasts and achieves high.

Another lesson learned from this experience was in the way the new plan was implemented. Because the sales force consisted of only twelve people, the owner-CEO told them as a group he was unhappy, listened to their complaints and suggestions, returned with a draft, and then met with each salesperson individually to refine the plan further. The result was a participatively created and accepted program which worked.

Issue 17

"How do you get people to do the job you know they are capable of doing?"

COMMENT

You cannot compel people to do things, they do them on their own initiative. The approach one small company owner-manager took was simply to tell people "why." We often assume that because we have the big picture and know the reason for a piece of work, the employee does also. Telling him why implies that the employee wants to know and will use his discretion to get the job done to satisfy the need.

Take the simple example: "I need this report by 5 P.M." The possibility that the job will be done and that the secretary will feel she is part of the picture will be enhanced if you add, "I have to leave for the airport by five o'clock" or "If we get the report out by five, we have a chance to get a new customer and open up a whole new market." If the explanation falls on uncaring ears, you have lost little. However, the odds are about 50 to 1 that adding "why" to a request will improve performance (which is the end result of motivation) and the boss-subordinate relationship.

Issue 18

Selection is consistently mentioned as one of the toughest personnel tasks.

COMMENT

The most frequently mentioned solution to improving selection is to use a competent industrial psychologist who learns your company's style, working environment, and interpersonal relations, and can match the applicant's skills and traits to the needs of the company and the group.

To that we add: Don't make selection tougher than it needs to be by expecting it to be a highly controllable process. At its best it is not. All you can do is raise the probabilities of making good selections from raw chance (one out of two) to about two out of three. Bad selections take place even in companies that are most diligent with respect to hiring. Thus, about all that can be done in respect to selection is to raise the results overall; there is no way to raise the probabilities on an individual selection.

Issue 19

"We see and hear a lot about people not wanting to work any more—the quality of work seems to have declined."

COMMENT

Murray Raphel, owner-manager of the highly successful Gordon's Alley, a group of stores in Atlantic City, New Jersey, offers several answers to this problem. Work standards are set by the people on top. If *they* work with a sense of the value of the job, if they respect the company and its assets (including their own time), and if they make clear to their subordinates what they want and then show that they care about the results by sensitive checking-up and offering praise for work well done, they will be able to increase the quality of work and results.

Involvement does not mean turning over managerial responsibilities which cannot be delegated. It does mean that you explain what you intend to do: either to ask opinions or just as a courtesy. Studies have shown that most people do *not* want the responsibility for decisions that affect them. They are willing to leave that to the manager. However, they do want to participate and provide input.

Consultative management is generally more acceptable than is participative management in most hierarchical organizations. In companies with shallow organizations (most professional and technological firms), participative management is more likely to be successful. Otherwise, respect people by asking and telling them; but don't be disappointed when they leave you to make the final decision.

Murray Raphel expresses his thanks to his employees for making the business successful every evening, and once a year he closes the stores and takes *everyone* away for a two-day, all-expense-paid vacation.

Issue 20

A company that employed a large number of low-skill people was concerned with resisting attempts at unionization. The company had barely won several organizing elections. The problem was the first task assigned to a new personnel director.

COMMENT

To introduce himself, the personnel director scheduled conferences with each employee to learn his or her perception of job problems and to get to know them individually. The union was not mentioned. The result: the union made organizing attempts the following year, but it was defeated by an even greater majority.

Although a personnel director cannot be the sole source for dealing with daily concerns affecting personnel issues, such as productivity, training, new methods, and personnel development, the personnel manager in this case did three things that improved conditions:

1. He eliminated the third shift, source of most turnover. By more careful scheduling of fixed asset capacity on the first two shifts, the savings from reduced personnel turnover were greater than the loss in third-shift production.

2. He established regular group meetings of foremen with their subordinates on company time as an escape valve for complaints and incipient problems. The meetings were only one visible sign of the company's intent to communicate in both directions. In addition to listening, foremen explained the company's plans. A newspaper, bulletin board, suggestion box, departmental representation on a plant council, and an annual presentation by the CEO at the plant picnic all reinforced the expanded communications policy.

3. He trained foremen to be supervisors. Senior management had believed that managers were born, not made, and that the good worker who was promoted to foreman would use supervisory skills copied from existing models—his own superiors—or, if he was a strong person, would draw from his own experience and values. Unwilling to take the risk of that random and inconsistent approach, the personnel manager convinced top

management to invest in training foremen toward a constant model.

Issue 21

A natural resources company has thirty plant locations in ten states, employing low-skill, minimum-wage-level workers. Except for two large installations, the plants have an average of thirty people, insufficient to justify on-site personnel managers. How can a company so decentralized support a professional personnel function to handle local problems, resist unionization, and reduce turnover caused by wage competition?

COMMENT

The company applied several solutions to the problem. They viewed personnel as a function to be exercised professionally throughout the company within the constraints of the economics of travel and the number of affordable people. They ranked their personnel manager high enough in the organization that he participated in the making of key management decisions and policies. In that way, the influence of their personnel professional was felt throughout the company, in addition to his direct responsibility for the more obvious areas of wages, fringe benefits, and regulatory compliance.

By constant reinforcement of personnel policies with the operating supervisors who had to travel, the personnel manager was able to keep personnel policies consistent. He also appointed a supervisor at each location to be responsible for selection, interpreting of fringe benefits, and identification of incipient problems. The supervisors were brought together regionally each quarter for training and discussion. Personnel training was supported by regular in-house bulletins and subscriptions to supervisory magazines. The cost was minimal. The result was uniform policies where they counted and individual policies for a plant where they made sense. The importance of the personnel function was shown by its visibility.

Issue 22

"How do you control turnover when you are paying minimal wages and fringes and the work is inherently dull?"

COMMENT

When people are earning minimum salaries they are constantly concerned with life necessities and it is unrealistic not to include money in your motivational tools. *If* the job can be expanded and satisfaction enhanced, expand it. But some jobs are inherently and unchangeably dull and repetitive. Accept their dullness, and hire people who will accept the job because their employment choices are limited. Saul Gellerman said it best: Hire dull people for dull jobs and give them opportunities for social relationships.

In this specific case, the company expanded hiring to include people with below-average intelligence (as shown in simple tests) who had previously never been thought of as potential employees. The company was in the south, and all manual work, even light tasks such as applying labels, cleanup, and forklift driving, had traditionally been done only by white men. Through careful screening, the personnel manager was able to hire the right people for the work and reduce turnover.

More directly, the company pays a bonus for people who show up regularly. At Christmas, if the employee is still working for the company, he can redeem $2 certificates distributed with each paycheck for perfect weekly attendance. An employee earns a one-week vacation (the only vacation given) if his attendance record is 98 percent for the prior year. Weekly, perfect attendance is recognized by posting gold stars next to the names by the time clock.

Many managers will react negatively to such solutions. Do you reward people for doing what they are being paid for—showing up and working? Can you run a business today by offering a one-week vacation only for 98 percent attendance and not for longevity? Is $104 paid at Christmas enough to get someone to come to work regularly? The answers are yes, when the circumstances are right.

What worked in attracting and retaining people in low-level, repetitive jobs in a backwoods operation is not the same as what will work at IBM or Eastman Kodak. But, this *is* a backwoods operation, and the CEO and personnel manager of this company are starting to improve results by employing such personnel practices. They are listening, they are being more selective in hiring, and they are reinforcing the behavior they want with modest rewards. The results show their actions are working: turnover is down, productivity is up, and three attempts at unionization have been defeated.

They have also been helped by the relative lack of other job opportunities. Most rural plant workers continue to work their marginal farms before and after the forty-hour work week. To them, the plant wages are a plus, minimum or not.

Appendix

Attitude Survey

1. How do you feel about your job?
   Good _____   OK _____   Poor _____
2. What could the company do to make your job more interesting?
   _____
   _____

3. How do you feel about your immediate supervisor?
   Good _____   OK _____
   Poor _____   No Comment _____
4. What are your feelings about the company as a place to work?
   _____
   _____

5. What is the best thing about working for the company?
   _____
   _____

6. If you were running the company, what is the first thing you
   would change and how would you do it?
   _____
   _____
   _____

7. Who is the most effective supervisor you know?
   _____

8. What job at the company would you like better than the one
   you have now?
   _____

9. Where do you think the company will be five years from now?
   Questionable _____   Expanding _____
   No comment _____   Out of Business _____

Compensation Survey

1. How would you describe the Company's management style?
   Relaxed _____ Pressured _____
   Demanding _____ Other _____

2. What is the present compensation plan in your company?
   _____
   _____
   _____

3. Do you know why you received the specific amount of your last salary increase? Yes _____ No _____
   Why?_____
   _____

4. What do you have to do to receive an improvement in compensation? _____
   _____
   _____

5. Does the compensation plan now in effect motivate you to assume greater responsibilities or to take risks in your decision-making? Yes _____ No _____
   How? _____
   _____

6. Does the current compensation plan motivate others toward better performance? Yes _____ No _____
   How? _____
   _____
   _____

7. How much control do you have over the factors that determine whether you're doing a good job?
   _____
   _____

8. With *one* as the most important, rank the five people who contribute the most to the company's success. Consider *every-*

one including yourself. 1. _____ 2. _____
3. _____ 4. _____ 5. _____

9. Are there any parts of the fringe benefit program you do not understand? Yes _____ No _____
What are they? _____

_____

_____

10. Overall, how do you rate the present fringe benefit program?
Excellent _____ Good _____ Fair _____
Comments: _____

_____

11. On a scale where ten is the highest, what number represents how the company is using your capabilities and skills? _____

12. Does the company share with you your contributions to its profit? Yes _____ No _____
How? _____

_____

13. Is the lack of information about the business preventing you from doing a better job? Yes _____ No_____
What information? _____

_____

_____

14. How do you know when you have done a good job?

_____

_____

Employee Survey

1. How do you feel layoffs are handled for employees like yourself?

I don't know	_____0
In the fairest possible way	_____1
In a reasonably fair way	_____2
In a partially fair and partially unfair way	_____3
In an unfair way	_____4

2. How do you feel about the way promotions and up-grades for employees like yourself are handled around here?

I don't know	_____0
Almost always handled fairly	_____1
Usually handled fairly	_____2
Usually not handled fairly	_____3
Hardly ever handled fairly	_____4

3. Overall, when you think about the way management communicates with employees here, which statement most closely fits your opinion?

Management is almost always frank and honest	_____1
Management is usually frank and honest	_____2
Management is usually not frank and honest	_____3
Management is almost always not frank and honest	_____4

4. When you discuss problems or complaints with your foreman or supervisor, how fairly are you treated?

I haven't had occasion to discuss problems or complaints with my foreman or supervisor	_____0
I am almost always treated fairly	_____1
I am usually treated fairly	_____2
I am usually not treated fairly	_____3
I am hardly ever treated fairly	_____4

5. My feelings about management's treatment of employees here are:

Employees are almost always treated fairly by management ____1

Employees are usually treated fairly by management ____2

Employees are usually not treated fairly by management ____3

Employees are hardly ever treated fairly by management ____4

6. Which of the following best describes your opinion of your present pay?

I don't know whether my pay is right for the work I do ____0

My pay is high for the work I do ____1

My pay is about right for the work I do ____2

My pay is low for the work I do, but I am not seriously concerned about it ____3

My pay is low for the work I do, and I *am* seriously concerned about it ____4

7. During the past year, would you say relationships between management and employees here have been getting better, getting worse, or have stayed about the same?

I don't know ____0

Getting better ____1

Staying about the same ____2

Getting worse ____3

8. If you do not receive a satisfactory answer to a complaint or problem from your immediate manager, how free do you feel to discuss the matter with someone else in the company?

Since I've had no problems that couldn't be solved by my manager, there has been no need to consider going to Employee Relations ____0

I almost always feel free to do this ____1

I usually feel free to do this ____2

I usually do not feel free to do this ____3

I hardly ever feel free to do this ____4

9. The promotion policy here places the most emphasis on:

I don't know ____0

Performance on the present job ____1

Qualifications and background for the new job ____2

Length of service ____3

Knowing or being known by the right people ____4

Other ____5

10. From past experience, I have learned that you can almost always count on management to keep its promises to employees. Do you agree or disagree?

    I have no experience to go on in answering this
        question   ____0
    Definitely agree   ____1
    Inclined to agree   ____2
    Inclined to disagree   ____3
    Definitely disagree   ____4

11. How long ago did you receive your last salary increase here?

    I have never received an increase here   ____0
    Within the past 12 months   ____1
    Between 12 and 18 months ago   ____2
    Between 18 and 24 months ago   ____3
    Over 24 months ago   ____4

12. In your opinion, how does your pay compare to wages paid for similar (or comparable) jobs in other companies in this community or area?

    I don't know how it compares   ____0
    My pay is higher than the average   ____1
    My pay is about average   ____2
    My pay is somewhat lower than the average   ____3
    My pay is quite a bit lower than the average   ____4

13. In general, when an employee breaks a work rule around here, is the disciplinary action (if any) too harsh, too lenient, or about right?

    I don't know   ____0
    It is too harsh   ____1
    It is about right   ____2
    It is too lenient   ____3
    No action is taken   ____4

14. How can our plant be made a better place to work? Write your suggestions.

_____

_____

_____

_____

_____

Personnel Survey

1. How do you feel when you tell people what firm you work for?
   a. Proud _____
   b. Good _____
   c. Just a place to work _____

2. Do you think the firm offers you the chance to have the kind of job that you will want five years from now?
   a. Yes _____
   b. No _____
   c. Not sure _____

3. To what extent are you made to feel that you are really a part of the firm?
   a. Not at all _____
   b. To a small degree _____
   c. To a large degree _____
   d. In every possible way _____

4. Do you feel that favoritism (in making assignments, giving raises and promotions) is shown in the firm?
   a. None _____
   b. Very little _____
   c. Some _____
   d. Much _____

5. To what extent do you understand just what work you are supposed to do and what your duties are?
   a. Very poor understanding _____
   b. Fairly good understanding _____
   c. Clear understanding _____

6. Do your supervisors on the job set a good example in their own work habits?
   a. All of them do _____
   b. Most of them do _____
   c. Some of them do _____
   d. None of them do _____

7. When you want information or help on a difficult problem, how likely are you to get the help you need? I get:
   a. Very little help _____

b. Fairly good help ____
c. All the help I need ____

8. When changes are made in the work you have done, how often are you told the reason for the change?
    a. Rarely ____
    b. Sometimes ____
    c. Usually ____
    d. Always ____

9. When you are corrected or when your work is being criticized, how often is this done in a way helpful to you?
    a. Sometimes ____
    b. Usually ____
    c. Always ____

10. Do you find the work assigned to you challenging and interesting?
    a. Sometimes ____
    b. Usually ____
    c. Always ____

11. Are you encouraged to offer ideas and suggestions for new or better ways of doing things?
    a. All the time ____
    b. Often ____
    c. Sometimes ____
    d. Rarely ____
    e. Not at all ____

12. What progress have you made with the firm?
    a. Excellent ____
    b. Satisfactory ____
    c. Some ____
    d. Little ____
    e. None ____

13. In general, how well do you like your present position?
    a. I like it very much ____
    b. I am satisfied with it ____
    c. I neither like nor dislike it ____
    d. I dislike it ____

14. How do you believe you are paid relative to your worth to the company?
    a. Very fair ____
    b. Adequately ____
    c. Unfairly ____

15. How do you believe you are compensated relative to others in the company?
    a. Very fairly _____
    b. Adequately _____
    c. Unfairly _____

16. In general, how do you feel about the workload expected of you?
    a. I should like to have more work to do _____
    b. The amount of work expected is reasonable _____
    c. The amount of work expected is somewhat too great _____
    d. The amount of work expected is unreasonable _____

17. How do you rate the policies on vacation, holidays, and other payments for time not worked?
    a. Excellent _____
    b. Good _____
    c. Fair _____
    d. Poor _____

18. How do you rate the policies on group medical insurance, life insurance, and similar benefits?
    a. Excellent _____
    b. Good _____
    c. Fair _____
    d. Poor _____

19. What attention will your personal problems be given if you bring them to the firm's attention?
    a. Substantial attention _____
    b. Some attention _____
    c. Not much attention _____

20. What opportunity for advancement do you have in the firm?
    a. Much opportunity _____
    b. Some opportunity _____
    c. Little opportunity _____
    d. No opportunity _____

21. When you were interviewed for employment, were the opportunities described fairly and honestly?
    a. Not as good as described _____
    b. Fairly and honestly described _____
    c. Somewhat better than described _____
    d. Much better than described _____

22. When you started to work for the firm, how were the training and help you received?

a. More than I needed _____
b. All I needed _____
c. Almost all I needed _____
d. Less than I needed _____
e. Very little _____

23. Does the firm keep you informed about its activities and plans?
    a. Always _____
    b. Usually _____
    c. Sometimes _____
    d. Seldom _____
    e. Never _____

24. As far as you can see, are the main decisions of the company generally made on the basis of the needs of the firm or according to private judgment and interest?
    a. According to the needs of the firm _____
    b. According to private judgment and interest _____

25. In your opinion, is management of the firm primarily client/customer-oriented or does it primarily serve the interests of the owners?
    a. Primarily client/customer-oriented _____
    b. Primarily serves owners' interests _____

26. As far as you can see, are employees treated as being basically intelligent, capable, and willing—or, as being unreliable and not intelligent?
    a. Intelligent and capable _____
    b. No consistent treatment _____
    c. Unreliable and not intelligent _____

27. Is your performance measured against some standard you know in advance, or on the basis of someone's opinion?
    a. Performance judged against standards _____
    b. Performance judged on basis of opinion _____

28. Are employees promoted or given pay increases because of what they contribute to the company, or because of other reasons?
    a. According to contribution _____
    b. Other reasons _____

29. Is management willing to share the contributions to profit made by employees?
    a. Yes _____
    b. No _____

30. On a scale where 10 is the highest use of your abilities and

skills, what number represents the way the company is using *your* capabilities and skills? _____

31. How do most employees feel about the firm?
    a. They are loyal and conscientious _____
    b. They are indifferent _____
    c. They really don't care _____

32. Is the management atmosphere in the company open with sharing of views, information, and power—or is it secret and closed, with information withheld?
    a. An open, frank atmosphere _____
    b. A closed, withholding atmosphere _____

33. Considering the opportunities which were available to you, do you now feel that you chose the right job?
    a. I prefer this job to any other _____
    b. I like this job better than most others _____
    c. I sometimes wish I had chosen some other job _____
    d. I definitely wish I had chosen some other job _____

34. If you were to start again, do you feel you would go to work with our firm?
    a. Yes _____
    b. No _____
    c. Don't know

35. What do you think of this opinion poll?
    a. I like it _____
    b. Probably all right _____
    c. I don't like it _____

36. What can be done to improve the performance and/or working conditions in the company? Mark those of the following needing considerable improvement:
    a. More clearly defined goals _____
    b. Better internal communications _____
    c. Better company planning _____
    d. More frequent staff meetings _____
    e. Improved understanding of each person's responsibilities
       _____
    f. Improved physical surroundings _____
    g. More sensitivity to customer/client needs _____
    h. Sound, fair performance standards _____
    i. More qualified people _____
    j. Better employee indoctrination and training _____
    k. Improved staff productivity _____
    l. More or better equipment _____

m. More regular and factual salary review _____
n. Broader participation in decision-making _____
o. More room for development and advancement _____
p. Other _____
_____
_____

Please answer the following:

_____Male   _____Female
Number of years with company: (1) Less than 1 year _____
                               (2)   1 to 3 years _____

                               (3)   4 to 6 years _____

                               (4)   Over 7 years _____

Department _____

Opinion Survey

1. How would you rate the firm as a company to work for compared with other companies you know about? CHOOSE ONE:
   - a. One of the best
   - b. Above average
   - c. Average
   - d. Below average
   - e. One of the worst

2. If you have your own way, will you be working for the company *5 years* from now? CHOOSE ONE:
   - a. Certainly
   - b. Probably
   - c. Not sure
   - d. Probably not
   - e. Certainly not
   - f. I'll be retired by then

3. How would you rate your "security" to continue working for the firm as long as you perform satisfactorily? CHOOSE ONE:
   - a. Very good
   - b. Good
   - c. Average
   - d. Poor
   - e. Very poor

4. How would you rate your "security" that you will not be transferred to a lower job (less skills, less responsibility, etc.)? CHOOSE ONE:
   - a. Very good
   - b. Good
   - c. Average
   - d. Poor
   - e. Very poor

5. How would you rate the adequacy of the total company benefits package? CHOOSE ONE:
   - a. Very good
   - b. Good

    c . Average

    d. Poor

    e . Very poor

6. If you were to start again, would you work for this firm again?

    a . Yes

    b. No

    c . I don't know

7. To what extent do you feel that you and the people in your work group belong to a team that works together? CHOOSE ONE:

    a . To a very great extent, I feel that we belong to a team.

    b. To a considerable extent

    c . To some extent

    d. To a little extent

    e . To no extent

8. How would you rate your physical working conditions (heat, noise, light, cleanliness, etc.)? CHOOSE ONE:

    a . Very good

    b. Good

    c . Average

    d. Poor

    e . Very poor

9. How would you rate the safety and health conditions in locations at which you work? CHOOSE ONE:

    a . Very good

    b. Good

    c . Average

    d. Poor

    e . Very poor

10. How would you rate your pay (total earnings) considering your duties and responsibilities? CHOOSE ONE:

    a . Very good

    b. Good

    c . Average

    d. Poor

    e . Very poor

11. How would you rate your pay (total earnings) considering what you could get for the same kind of work in other companies? CHOOSE ONE:

    a . Very good

    b. Good

    c . Average

d. Poor

e. Very poor

12. To what extent do you personally agree or disagree with the following statement? CHOOSE ONE:

    The better my performance, the more money I will make.
    a. Strongly agree
    b. Agree
    c. Neither agree nor disagree
    d. Disagree
    e. Strongly disagree

13. Do your supervisors on the job set a good example in their own work habits? CHOOSE ONE:
    a. All of them do
    b. Most of them do
    c. Some of them do
    d. None of them do

14. How do you like your job—the kind of work you do? CHOOSE ONE:
    a. Very good
    b. Good
    c. Average
    d. Poor
    e. Very poor

15. How often is good use made of your skills and abilities in your present job? CHOOSE ONE:
    a. Always
    b. Usually
    c. Sometimes
    d. Seldom
    e. Never

16. How do you feel when you tell people what company you work for? CHOOSE ONE:
    a. Proud
    b. Good
    c. Just a place to work

17. How do you know when you've done a good job? CHOOSE ONE:
    a. Supervisor tells me
    b. I meet performance goals
    c. No one criticized me
    d. I know in my own heart
    e. I don't know

18. How does management treat employees? CHOOSE ONE OR MORE:

Your Super- visor	*Top Manage- ment*	
_____	_____	As though they can be trusted
_____	_____	With respect
_____	_____	With concern for each person as an individual
_____	_____	Just a pair of hands
_____	_____	A necessary means to make a profit
_____	_____	As though they cannot be trusted

Listed below are various kinds of problems that may or may not arise in your work. Please indicate to what extent you find each of the following to be a problem, concern, or obstacle in carrying out your duties and responsibilities. CHOOSE ONE IN EACH ROW:

	Never	*Seldom*	*Sometimes*	*Often*	*Always*
19. Being unclear on just what the scope and respon- sibilities of your job are	1	2	3	4	5
20. The fact that you can't get informa- tion needed to carry out your job	1	2	3	4	5
21. Having a lot of red tape involved in getting a job done	1	2	3	4	5

How satisfied are you in your job with each of the following? CHOOSE ONE IN EACH ROW:

	Very Satisfied	*Satisfied*	*Neither Satisfied nor Dissatisfied*	*Dissatisfied*	*Very Dissatisfied*
22. The freedom you have to adopt your own ap- proach to the job	1	2	3	4	5
23. The efficiency with which your department is run	1	2	3	4	5
24. The recognition you get when you do a good job	1	2	3	4	5

	Very Satisfied	Satisfied	Neither Satisfied nor Dissatisfied	Dissatisfied	Very Dissatisfied

25. The challenge of the work you do—the extent to which you can get a personal sense of accomplishment from it   1   2   3   4   5

26. How do you feel about the amount of work you are expected to do? CHOOSE ONE:
    a. Too much
    b. About the right amount
    c. I would prefer to do more

27. On the job do you feel any pressure for increasing your output above what you think is reasonable? CHOOSE ONE:
    a. A great deal of pressure
    b. Quite a bit of pressure
    c. Some pressure
    d. A little pressure
    e. No pressure at all

28. In recent months have job pressure or requirements interfered with your personal or family life? CHOOSE ONE:
    a. Yes, very often
    b. Quite often
    c. Sometimes
    d. Seldom
    e. Never

29. How good a job do you feel is being done by your immediate manager? CHOOSE ONE:
    a. Very good
    b. Good
    c. So-so
    d. Poor
    e. Very poor
    f. I know nothing about the job done at this level.

30. How much trust and confidence do you have in your immediate manager? CHOOSE ONE:
    a. A great deal
    b. Quite a bit
    c. Some
    d. A little
    e. Very little or none

31. To what extent is there effective two-way communication be-
    tween you and your immediate manager? CHOOSE ONE:
    a. To a very great extent
    b. To a considerable extent
    c. To some extent
    d. To a little extent
    e. To no extent

Overall, how would you rate your immediate manager in terms of
each of the following? CHOOSE ONE IN EACH ROW:

	Very Good	Good	Average	Poor	Very Poor
32. Ability to manage his work	1	2	3	4	5
33. Ability to manage people responsibilities	1	2	3	4	5

34. How satisfied are you with the accuracy of your last perfor-
    mance rating? CHOOSE ONE:
    a. Very satisfied
    b. Satisifed
    c. Neither satisfied nor dissatisfied
    d. Dissatisfied
    e. Very dissatisfied
    f. I've never been appraised

The statements below describe various things a manager may or
may not do. Each statement asks only for a judgment of how typical
this behavior is of your immediate manager; it does not call for
your evaluation of whether the behavior is desirable or undesirable. You are, therefore, being asked only to describe how often
your immediate manager does the various things mentioned in
the list. CHOOSE THE NUMBER IN EACH ROW WHICH
SEEMS TO FIT BEST:

	Never	Very Infre-quently	Infre-quently	About as Often as not	Fre-quently	Very Fre-quently	Always
How often does your immediate manager do this?							
35. Keeps you informed on matters affecting you and your work	1	2	3	4	5	6	7

	Never	Very Infre- quently	Infre- quently	About as Often as not	Fre- quently	Very Fre- quently	Always
36. Is friendly in dealing with you	1	2	3	4	5	6	7
37. Asks for your partic- ipation in establishing goals and schedules that pertain to your work	1	2	3	4	5	6	7
38. Is able to give you competent help in your work when you ask for it	1	2	3	4	5	6	7
39. Is willing to listen to your ideas and suggestions	1	2	3	4	5	6	7

How good a job do you think is being done by each of the following levels of management? CHOOSE ONE IN EACH ROW:

	Very Good	Good	Average	Poor	Very Poor	I know nothing about the job done at this level
40. The person who su- pervises your manager	1	2	3	4	5	6
41. The company's top management	1	2	3	4	5	6

42. Does management spend its time effectively to help the company? CHOOSE ONE:
a. Always
b. Usually
c. Rarely
d. Don't know

The statements below describe various things a manager may or may not do. Each statement asks only for a judgment of how typical this behavior is of your immediate *manager's manager;* it does not call for your evaluation of whether the behavior is desirable or undesirable. You are, therefore, being asked only to describe how often your immediate *manager's manager* does the various things mentioned in the list. CHOOSE THE NUMBER IN EACH ROW WHICH SEEMS TO FIT BEST:

	Never	Very Infre- quently	Infre- quently	About as Often as not	Fre- quently	Very Fre- quently	Always
How often does your *manager's manager* do this?							
43. Is friendly in dealing with you	1	2	3	4	5	6	7
44. Keeps you informed on matters affecting you and your work	1	2	3	4	5	6	7

45. Suppose you felt you were being treated unfairly on some particular issue that was important to you, and you had been unsuccessful in correcting it through your manager. Do you think it would help to take your complaint to higher management? CHOOSE ONE:
 a. Yes, this definitely would help.
 b. Yes, this probably would help.
 c. No, this probably would not help.
 d. No, this definitely would not help.

46. Now suppose you did take such a complaint to higher management after having taken it up with your manager. Do you think you would be hurt later for doing this? (Get less-desirable jobs; be held back on salary increases, etc.) CHOOSE ONE:
 a. No, I would definitely not be hurt for doing this.
 b. No, probably not.
 c. Yes, probably.
 d. Yes, I would definitely be hurt for doing this.

Please indicate the extent to which you personally agree or disagree with the following statements. CHOOSE ONE IN EACH ROW:

	Strongly Agree	Agree	Neither Agree nor Disagree	Disagree	Strongly Disagree
47. My immediate boss makes himself aware of the problems of people	1	2	3	4	5
48. Top management acts to clear up the problems of people	1	2	3	4	5

49. Do you feel that the results of surveys such as this one will be used constructively by your management? CHOOSE ONE:
    a. Yes, definitely
    b. Yes, probably
    c. No, probably not
    d. No, definitely not

50. As far as you know, were conditions improved as a result of any previous survey? CHOOSE ONE:
    a. Yes, a great deal of improvement was made.
    b. Quite a bit
    c. Some
    d. Just a little
    e. As far as I know, no improvements were made as a result of the previous Opinion Survey.
    f. I did not participate in the previous survey.

51. How would you rate your opportunity to move to a better job in the company? CHOOSE ONE:
    a. Very good
    b. Good
    c. Average
    d. Poor
    e. Very poor

52. To what extent do you personally agree or disagree with the following statement? CHOOSE ONE:

    "The better my performance, the greater will be my opportunity for advancement."
    a. Strongly agree
    b. Agree

   c. Neither agree nor disagree

   d. Disagree

   e. Strongly disagree

53. How satisfied are you with the various activities (job training, education programs, seminars, etc.) made available to assist you in your personal/career development? CHOOSE ONE:

   a. Very satisfied

   b. Satisfied

   c. Neither satisfied nor dissatisfied

   d. Dissatisfied

   e. Very dissatisfied

To what extent do you personally agree or disagree with the following statements? CHOOSE ONE IN EACH ROW:

	Strongly Agree	Agree	Neither Agree nor Disagree	Disagree	Strongly Disagree
54. Management effectively carries out a commitment to Equal Opportunity	1	2	3	4	5
55. I am familiar with the company's Equal Opportunity Program	1	2	3	4	5
56. I fully support the company's commitment to Equal Opportunity	1	2	3	4	5
57. I feel that the company's efforts in the Equal Opportunity area are fairly implemented	1	2	3	4	5

58. Considering everything, how would you rate *your* overall satisfaction in the company at the present time? CHOOSE ONE:

   a. Completely satisfied

   b. Very satisfied

   c. Satisfied

   d. Neither satisfied nor dissatisfied

   e. Dissatisfied

   f. Very dissatisfied

   g. Completely dissatisfied

59. Considering everything, how would you rate the overall satisfaction of *everyone* in the company at the present time? CHOOSE ONE:
    a. Completely satisfied
    b. Very satisfied
    c. Satisfied
    d. Neither satisfied nor dissatisfied
    e. Dissatisfied
    f. Very dissatisfied
    g. Completely dissatisfied

60. Who comes first in the way the company is run? CHOOSE ONE:
    a. Customers
    b. Owners
    c. The company itself
    d. Everyone for himself
    e. Don't know

To what extent do the following affect your work? CHOOSE ONE IN EACH ROW:

	To a Great Extent	To a Considerable Extent	To Some Extent	To a Little Extent	To No Extent
61. Lack of responsiveness from other people *within* my office or work group	1	2	3	4	5
62. Inadequate managerial support	1	2	3	4	5
63. Inadequate manpower *within* my office	1	2	3	4	5
64. Low supervisory experience *within* my office	1	2	3	4	5
65. Inadequate instructions about new procedures on my job	1	2	3	4	5

To what extent do you personally agree/disagree with the following statements? CHOOSE ONE IN EACH ROW:

	Strongly Agree	Agree	Neither Agree nor Disagree	Disagree	Strongly Disagree
66. Management recognizes accomplishments I make on my job	1	2	3	4	5
67. My job allows me to improve my present skills and learn new skills	1	2	3	4	5
68. I know what I must accomplish to improve my performance	1	2	3	4	5

69. Are people more likely to be criticized for poor performance than recognized for good performance?
    a. More likely criticized
    b. More likely recognized

70. If you are working 12 months from now, and you have your own way, will you be working for the company? CHOOSE ONE:
    a. Certainly
    b. Probably
    c. Not sure
    d. Probably not
    e. Certainly not
    f. I will not be working 12 months from now.

How often are the following true? CHOOSE ONE IN EACH ROW:

	Always	Usually	Sometimes	Seldom	Never
71. Job-related information gets to you when you need it	1	2	3	4	5
72. Everyone is doing a fair share of the work	1	2	3	4	5

73. To what extent do you agree that in order for the company to pay higher wages each year, it is necessary to find ways of increasing productivity? CHOOSE ONE:
    a. Strongly agree
    b. Agree
    c. Neither agree nor disagree
    d. Disagree
    e. Strongly disagree

74. If conditions were ideal (good supplies, good organization, good supervision, good procedures, good rewards, etc.), how much would you say you could increase your productivity? CHOOSE ONE:
    a. Not at all—my productivity is about as high as it could be.
    b. If conditions were ideal, I could probably increase my productivity 1–5%.
    c. 6–15%
    d. 16–25%
    e. 26–50%
    f. More than 50%

75. If there is a conflict between quality and production standards, how would most of the people in the company decide? CHOOSE ONE:
    a. For top quality
    b. For highest production
    c. Don't know
    d. Don't care

76. How do you feel about the amount of overtime you have worked during the past three months? CHOOSE ONE:
    a. Too much
    b. About the right amount
    c. Would prefer more
    d. I have had no overtime

77. On a scale of 1 to 10 where 10 is most honest, at what level of honesty do you think the people in this company are operating? _____(Enter a number from 1 to 10.)

    For each of the following methods of training you may have received during the past 12 months, indicate how effective that training was. CHOOSE ONE IN EACH ROW:

	Very Good	Good	Average	Poor	Very Poor	Did not receive this kind of Training
78. New Employee Orientation	1	2	3	4	5	6
79. Job Training by Manager	1	2	3	4	5	6
80. Job Training by Co-worker	1	2	3	4	5	6
81. Classroom Training	1	2	3	4	5	6
82. Advanced Seminar	1	2	3	4	5	6

83. How would you rate your opportunity to progress in the company in the next two years? CHOOSE ONE:
    a. Very good
    b. Good
    c. Average
    d. Poor
    e. Very poor

84. If you could do anything to improve the company, what 3 things would you do?
    a. _____
       _____
    b. _____
       _____
    c. _____
       _____

Background Information

The information which you provide in answering these questions is completely confidential. Your responses will be grouped statistically with those of the many other people who are participating in this survey.

A vital aspect of this survey consists of grouping data for people with varying amounts of previous experience and backgrounds. To do this, we need your answers to the following questions. *THIS MATERIAL WILL NOT BE PRINTED OUT IN ANY OF THE FEEDBACK REPORTS RECEIVED BY YOUR MANAGEMENT.*

85. How old are you?
    a. Under 20
    b. 20–24
    c. 25–29
    d. 30–34
    e. 35–39
    f. 40–44
    g. 45–49
    h. 50–54
    i. 55 & over

86. Are you: a. Man   b. Woman

87. How long have you been employed by the company? (Round off to the nearest month.)
    a. Less than 6 months
    b. Between 6 months and 1 year
    c. More than 1 year but less than 2 years
    d. Between 2 years and 4 years, 11 months

e. Between 5 years and 9 years, 11 months
f. Between 10 years and 14 years, 11 months
g. Between 15 years and 24 years, 11 months
h. 25 years or more

88. What was your last appraisal rating? CHOOSE ONE:
    a. Far exceeded requirements
    b. Consistently exceeded
    c. Exceeded at times
    d. Met requirements
    e. Unsatisfactory
    f. I don't know
    g. I've never been appraised in the company.

89. During the last 6 months, approximately how many hours have you worked during a typical or average week? CHOOSE ONE:
    a. Less than 40 hours
    b. 40 hours
    c. 41–45 hours
    d. 46–50 hours
    e. 51–55 hours
    f. More than 55 hours

This survey is modified and edited from several sources.

Index